The First Part of King Henry the Fourth

THE YALE SHAKESPEARE

EDITED BY

WILBUR L. CROSS   TUCKER BROOKE

WILLARD HIGLEY DURHAM

PUBLISHED UNDER THE DIRECTION

OF THE

DEPARTMENT OF ENGLISH, YALE UNIVERSITY,

ON THE FUND

GIVEN TO THE YALE UNIVERSITY PRESS IN 1917

BY MEMBERS OF THE

KINGSLEY TRUST ASSOCIATION

TO COMMEMORATE THE SEVENTY-FIFTH ANNIVERSARY

OF THE FOUNDING OF THE SOCIETY

The Yale Shakespeare

THE FIRST PART OF KING HENRY THE FOURTH

WITH THE LIFE AND DEATH OF HENRY, SURNAMED HOTSPUR

Shakespeare, William

EDITED BY
SAMUEL B. HEMINGWAY

NEW HAVEN · YALE UNIVERSITY PRESS
LONDON · HUMPHREY MILFORD
OXFORD UNIVERSITY PRESS · MCMXVII

TABLE OF CONTENTS

The map opposite represents the principal towns, rivers, etc., mentioned in "The First Part of King Henry the Fourth."

[DRAMATIS PERSONÆ

KING HENRY THE FOURTH
HENRY, *Prince of Wales,* }
JOHN OF LANCASTER, } *Sons to the King*
EARL OF WESTMORELAND
SIR WALTER BLUNT
THOMAS PERCY, *Earl of Worcester*
HENRY PERCY, *Earl of Northumberland*
HENRY PERCY *surnamed* HOTSPUR, *his son*
EDMUND MORTIMER, *Earl of March*
RICHARD SCROOP, *Archbishop of York*
ARCHIBALD, *Earl of Douglas*
OWEN GLENDOWER
SIR RICHARD VERNON
SIR JOHN FALSTAFF
SIR MICHAEL, *a Friend to the Archbishop of York*
POINS
GADSHILL
PETO
BARDOLPH
FRANCIS, *a Drawer*
LADY PERCY, *Wife to Hotspur, and Sister to Mortimer*
LADY MORTIMER, *Daughter to Glendower, and Wife to Mortimer*
MISTRESS QUICKLY, *Hostess of the Boar's Head Tavern in Eastcheap*

Lords, Officers, Sheriff, Vintner, Chamberlain, Drawers, two Carriers, Travellers, and Attendants

SCENE: *England.*]

The First Part of Henry the Fourth

WITH THE LIFE AND DEATH OF HENRY, SURNAMED HOTSPUR

ACT FIRST

Scene One

[London. The Palace]

Enter the King, Lord John of Lancaster, Earl of Westmoreland, with others.

King. So shaken as we are, so wan with care.
Find we a time for frighted peace to pant,
And breathe short-winded accents of new broils
To be commenc'd in stronds afar remote.   4
No more the thirsty entrance of this soil
Shall daub her lips with her own children's blood;
No more shall trenching war channel her fields,
Nor bruise her flowerets with the armed hoofs   8
Of hostile paces: those opposed eyes,
Which, like the meteors of a troubled heaven,
All of one nature, of one substance bred,
Did lately meet in the intestine shock   12
And furious close of civil butchery,
Shall now, in mutual well-beseeming ranks,
March all one way, and be no more oppos'd
Against acquaintance, kindred, and allies: 16
The edge of war, like an ill-sheathed knife,
No more shall cut his master. Therefore, friends,

stronds: *coasts*   5 *Cf. n.*
trenching: *trench-digging*   channel: *make channels in*
intestine: *internal, civil*   13 close: *grapple*
mutual well-beseeming ranks: *ranks which have, most properly, a common interest*

As far as to the sepulchre of Christ,—
Whose soldier now, under whose blessed cross   20
We are impressed and engag'd to fight,—
Forthwith a power of English shall we levy,
Whose arms were moulded in their mothers' womb
To chase these pagans in those holy fields   24
Over whose acres walk'd those blessed feet
Which fourteen hundred years ago were nail'd
For our advantage on the bitter cross.
But this our purpose now is twelve months old,   28
And bootless 'tis to tell you we will go:
Therefore we meet not now. Then let me hear
Of you, my gentle cousin Westmoreland,
What yesternight our council did decree   32
In forwarding this dear expedience.

   West. My liege, this haste was hot in question,
And many limits of the charge set down
But yesternight; when all athwart there came
A post from Wales loaden with heavy news;   37
Whose worst was, that the noble Mortimer,
Leading the men of Herefordshire to fight
Against the irregular and wild Glendower,   40
Was by the rude hands of that Welshman taken,
A thousand of his people butchered;
Upon whose dead corpse there was such misuse,
Such beastly shameless transformation   44
By those Welshwomen done, as may not be
Without much shame re-told or spoken of.

   King. It seems then that the tidings of this broil
Brake off our business for the Holy Land.   48

---

21 impressed: *compelled into service*   28 *Cf. n.*   29 bootless: *useless*
33 dear expedience: *important expedition*
34 hot in question: *in hot debate*   35 charge: *expense*
36 athwart: *from an unexpected quarter*   38 Mortimer; *cf. n.*
40 irregular: *lawless*

West. This, match'd with other, did, my gracious
   lord;
For more uneven and unwelcome news
Came from the north and thus it did import:
On Holy-rood day, the gallant Hotspur there,   52
Young Harry Percy and brave Archibald,
That ever-valiant and approved Scot,
At Holmedon met,
Where they did spend a sad and bloody hour;
As by discharge of their artillery,   57
And shape of likelihood, the news was told;
For he that brought them, in the very heat
And pride of their contention did take horse,   60
Uncertain of the issue any way.
   King. Here is a dear and true industrious friend,
Sir Walter Blunt, new lighted from his horse,
Stain'd with the variation of each soil   64
Betwixt that Holmedon and this seat of ours;
And he hath brought us smooth and welcome news.
The Earl of Douglas is discomfited;
Ten thousand bold Scots, two and twenty knights,   68
Balk'd in their own blood did Sir Walter see
On Holmedon's plains: of prisoners Hotspur took
Mordake the Earl of Fife, and eldest son
To beaten Douglas, and the Earls of Athol,   72
Of Murray, Angus, and Menteith.
And is not this an honourable spoil?
A gallant prize? ha, cousin, is it not?
   West. In faith,   76
It is a conquest for a prince to boast of.
   King. Yea, there thou mak'st me sad and mak'st
     me sin

49 match'd: *joined*   50 uneven: *disconcerting*
52 Holy-rood day; *cf. n.*   53 Harry Percy; *cf. n.*
54 approved: *well-tried*   58 shape of likelihood: *probability*
59 balk'd: *piled up* (?)   71 Mordake; *cf. n.*

In envy that my Lord Northumberland
Should be the father to so blest a son,   80
A son who is the theme of honour's tongue;
Amongst a grove the very straightest plant;
Who is sweet Fortune's minion and her pride:
Whilst I, by looking on the praise of him,   84
See riot and dishonour stain the brow
Of my young Harry.   O! that it could be prov'd
That some night-tripping fairy had exchang'd
In cradle-clothes our children where they lay,   88
And call'd mine Percy, his Plantagenet.
Then would I have his Harry, and he mine.
But let him from my thoughts.   What think you, coz,
Of this young Percy's pride? the prisoners,   92
Which he in this adventure hath surpris'd,
To his own use he keeps, and sends me word,
I shall have none but Mordake Earl of Fife.

   West. This   is   his   uncle's   teaching,   this   is
     Worcester,   96
Malevolent to you in all aspects;
Which makes him prune himself, and bristle up
The crest of youth against your dignity.

   King. But I have sent for him to answer this;   100
And for this cause a while we must neglect
Our holy purpose to Jerusalem.
Cousin, on Wednesday next our council we
Will hold at Windsor; so inform the lords: 104
But come yourself with speed to us again;
For more is to be said and to be done
Than out of anger can be uttered.

   West. I will, my liege.   ,   *Exeunt.*

83 minion: *darling*
91 coz: *cousin, used by the sovereign in addressing any nobleman*
91-95 *Cf. n.*   97 *Cf. n.*   107 uttered; *cf. n.*

Scene Two

[The Same]

Enter Henry, Prince of Wales, and Sir John Falstaff.

Fal. Now, Hal, what time of day is it, lad?

Prince. Thou art so fat-witted, with drinking of old sack, and unbuttoning thee after supper, and sleeping upon benches after noon, that thou hast forgotten to demand that truly which thou wouldst truly know. What a devil hast thou to do with the time of the day? unless hours were cups of sack, and minutes capons, and clocks the tongues of bawds, and dials the signs of leaping-houses, and the blessed sun himself a fair hot wench in flame-colour'd taffeta, I see no reason why thou shouldst be so superfluous to demand the time of the day.   13

Fal. Indeed, you come near me now, Hal; for we that take purses go by the moon and the seven stars, and not by Phœbus, he, 'that wandering knight so fair.' And, I prithee, sweet wag, when thou art king,—as, God save thy Grace,—majesty, I should say, for grace thou wilt have none,—   20

Prince. What! none?

Fal. No, by my troth; not so much as will serve to be prologue to an egg and butter.

Prince. Well, how then? come, roundly, roundly.   25

Fal. Marry, then, sweet wag, when thou art

3 sack: *sweet Spanish wine*   9 bawds: *panders*
10 leaping-houses: *brothels*   16 *Cf. n.*   19-33 *Cf. n.*
24 roundly: *plainly, to the point*
26 Marry: an interjection, *well;* originally an oath, *by the Virgin Mary*

king, let not us that are squires of the night's
body be called thieves of the day's beauty: let
us be Diana's foresters, gentlemen of the shade,
minions of the moon; and let men say, we be
men of good government, being governed as the
sea is, by our noble and chaste mistress the
moon, under whose countenance we steal. 33

Prince. Thou sayest well, and it holds well
too; for the fortune of us that are the moon's
men doth ebb and flow like the sea, being governed as the sea is, by the moon. As for proof
now: a purse of gold most resolutely snatched
on Monday night and most dissolutely spent on
Tuesday morning; got with swearing 'Lay by;'
and spent with crying 'Bring in:' now in as
low an ebb as the foot of the ladder, and by and
by in as high a flow as the ridge of the gallows.

Fal. By the Lord, thou sayest true, lad. And
is not my hostess of the tavern a most sweet
wench? 46

Prince. As the honey of Hybla, my old lad of
the castle. And is not a buff jerkin a most sweet
robe of durance? 49

Fal. How now, how now, mad wag! what,
in thy quips and thy quiddities? what a plague
have I to do with a buff jerkin? 52

Prince. Why, what a pox have I to do with
my hostess of the tavern?

Fal. Well, thou hast called her to a reckoning many a time and oft.

29 Diana's: *the moon's*   30 minions: *servants*
40 'Lay by': *address of highwaymen to their victims*
41 'Bring in': *a call for wine*
47 honey of Hybla: *Sicilian honey*   lad of the castle; *cf. Appendix*
48 buff jerkin: *leather jacket worn by sheriff's officers; cf. n.*
49 durance: *a stuff noted for its durability*
51 quips: *jests*   quiddities: *subtleties, puns*

Prince. Did I ever call for thee to pay thy part?

Fal. No; I'll give thee thy due, thou hast paid all there.   60

Prince. Yea, and elsewhere, so far as my coin would stretch; and where it would not, I have used my credit.

Fal. Yea, and so used it that, were it not here apparent that thou art heir apparent,—But, I prithee, sweet wag, shall there be gallows standing in England when thou art king, and resolution thus fobbed as it is with the rusty curb of old father antic the law? Do not thou, when thou art king, hang a thief.   70

Prince. No; thou shalt.

Fal. Shall I? O rare! By the Lord, I'll be a brave judge.   73

Prince. Thou judgest false already; I mean, thou shalt have the hanging of the thieves and so become a rare hangman.   76

Fal. Well, Hal, well; and in some sort it jumps with my humour as well as waiting in the court, I can tell you.

Prince. For obtaining of suits?   80

Fal. Yea, for obtaining of suits, whereof the hangman hath no lean wardrobe. 'Sblood, I am as melancholy as a gib cat, or a lugged bear.

Prince. Or an old lion, or a lover's lute.   84

Fal. Yea, or the drone of a Lincolnshire bagpipe.

67 resolution: *determination, boldness*
68 fobbed: *tricked*   69 antic: *buffoon*   73 brave: *fine*
78 jumps: *agrees*   humour: *temperament, inclination*
81 obtaining of suits: *the clothes of the criminal were the hangman's perquisite*
82 'Sblood: *God's blood*
83 gib cat: *tom cat*   lugged bear: *bear led by a rope*

Prince. What sayest thou to a hare, or the
melancholy of Moor-ditch?   88

Fal. Thou hast the most unsavory similes,
and art, indeed, the most comparative, rascal-
liest, sweet young prince; but, Hal, I prithee,
trouble me no more with vanity. I would to God
thou and I knew where a commodity of good
names were to be bought. An old lord of the
council rated me the other day in the street about
you, sir, but I marked him not; and yet he
talked very wisely, but I regarded him not; and
yet he talked wisely, and in the street too.   98

Prince. Thou didst well; for wisdom cries
out in the streets, and no man regards it.   100

Fal. O! thou hast damnable iteration, and
art indeed able to corrupt a saint. Thou hast
done much harm upon me, Hal; God forgive
thee for it! Before I knew thee, Hal, I knew
nothing; and now am I, if a man should speak
truly, little better than one of the wicked. I
must give over this life, and I will give it over;
by the Lord, an I do not, I am a villain: I'll be
damned for never a king's son in Christendom.

Prince. Where shall we take a purse to-
morrow, Jack?   111

Fal. 'Zounds! where thou wilt, lad, I'll make
one; an I do not, call me a villain and baffle me.

Prince. I see a good amendment of life in
thee; from praying to purse-taking.   115

87 hare; *cf. n.*   88 Moor-ditch; *cf. n.*
90 comparative: *witty*, i.e., *full of witty comparisons*
93 commodity: *supply*   101 damnable iteration; *cf. n.*
112 'Zounds: *God's wounds*
113 baffle: *hang by the heels (a punishment inflicted on recreant knights)*

Fal. Why, Hal, 'tis my vocation, Hal; 'tis no sin for a man to labour in his vocation.

Enter Poins.

Poins! Now shall we know if Gadshill have set a match. O! if men were to be saved by merit, what hole in hell were hot enough for him? This is the most omnipotent villain that ever cried 'Stand!' to a true man.　　　122

Prince. Good morrow, Ned.

Poins. Good morrow, sweet Hal. What says Monsieur Remorse? What says Sir John Sack-and-Sugar? Jack! how agrees the devil and thee about thy soul, that thou soldest him on Good-Friday last for a cup of Madeira and a cold capon's leg?　　　129

Prince. Sir John stands to his word, the devil shall have his bargain; for he was never yet a breaker of proverbs: he will give the devil his due.

Poins. Then art thou damned for keeping thy word with the devil.

Prince. Else he had been damned for cozening the devil.　　　136

Poins. But my lads, my lads, to-morrow morning, by four o'clock, early at Gadshill! There are pilgrims going to Canterbury with rich offerings, and traders riding to London with fat purses: I have vizards for you all; you have horses for yourselves. Gadshill lies to-night in Rochester; I have bespoke supper to-morrow night in Eastcheap: we may do it as secure as sleep. If you will go I will stuff your purses full

---

Gadshill; *cf. n.*　　set a match: *planned a robbery*
cozening: *cheating*　141 vizards: *masks*　144 Eastcheap; *cf. n.*

of crowns; if you will not, tarry at home and be hanged. 14?

Fal. Hear ye, Yedward: if I tarry at home and go not, I'll hang you for going.

Poins. You will, chops?

Fal. Hal, wilt thou make one?

Prince. Who, I rob? I a thief? not I, by my faith. 155

Fal. There's neither honesty, manhood, nor good fellowship in thee, nor thou camest not of the blood royal, if thou darest not stand for ten shillings. 157

Prince. Well, then, once in my days I'll be a madcap.

Fal. Why, that's well said. 160

Prince. Well, come what will, I'll tarry at home.

Fal. By the Lord, I'll be a traitor then, when thou art king. 164

Prince. I care not.

Poins. Sir John, I prithee, leave the prince and me alone: I will lay him down such reasons for this adventure that he shall go. 168

Fal. Well, God give thee the spirit of persuasion and him the ears of profiting, that what thou speakest may move, and what he hears may be believed, that the true prince may, for recreation sake, prove a false thief; for the poor abuses of the time want countenance. Farewell: you shall find me in Eastcheap. 17?

Prince. Farewell, thou latter spring! Farewell, All-hallown summer! [*Exit Falstaff.*]

150 chops: *fat face*
177 All-hallown summer: *All Saints' summer; cf. n.*

Poins. Now, my good sweet honey lord, ride with us to-morrow: I have a jest to execute that I cannot manage alone.   Falstaff, Bardolph, Peto, and Gadshill shall rob those men that we have already waylaid; yourself and I will not be there; and when they have the booty, if you and I do not rob them, cut this head from my shoulders.   185

Prince. But how shall we part with them in setting forth?

Poins. Why, we will set forth before or after them, and appoint them a place of meeting, wherein it is at our pleasure to fail; and then will they adventure upon the exploit themselves, which they shall have no sooner achieved but we'll set upon them.   193

Prince. Yea, but 'tis like that they will know us by our horses, by our habits, and by every other appointment, to be ourselves.   196

Poins. Tut! our horses they shall not see, I'll tie them in the wood; our vizards we will change after we leave them; and, sirrah, I have cases of buckram for the nonce, to inmask our noted outward garments.   201

Prince. Yea, but I doubt they will be too hard for us.

Poins. Well, for two of them, I know them to be as true-bred cowards as ever turned back; and for the third, if he fight longer than he sees reason, I'll forswear arms.   The virtue of this jest will be, the incomprehensible lies that this

95 habits: *clothes*   196 appointment: *equipment*   199 sirrah; *cf. n.*
00 cases of buckram: *cloaks of coarse linen*   for the nonce: *for the occasion*
01 noted: *well-known*   206 the third; *cf. n.*

same fat rogue will tell us when we meet at
supper: how thirty, at least, he fought with;
what wards, what blows, what extremities he
endured; and in the reproof of this lies the jest.

Prince. Well, I'll go with thee: provide us
all things necessary and meet me to-morrow
night in Eastcheap; there I'll sup. Farewell.

   Poins. Farewell, my lord.   *Exit Poins.*

   Prince. I know you all, and will awhile uphold   217
The unyok'd humour of your idleness:
Yet herein will I imitate the sun,
Who doth permit the base contagious clouds
To smother up his beauty from the world,   221
That when he please again to be himself,
Being wanted, he may be more wonder'd at,
By breaking through the foul and ugly mists
Of vapours that did seem to strangle him.   225
If all the year were playing holidays,
To sport would be as tedious as to work;
But when they seldom come, they wish'd for come,
And nothing pleaseth but rare accidents.   229
So, when this loose behaviour I throw off,
And pay the debt I never promised,
By how much better than my word I am   232
By so much shall I falsify men's hopes;
And like bright metal on a sullen ground,
My reformation, glittering o'er my fault,
Shall show more goodly and attract more eyes
Than that which hath no foil to set it off.   237
I'll so offend to make offence a skill;
Redeeming time when men think least I will.   *Exit.*

211 wards: *guards in fencing*   212 reproof: *refutation*
218 unyok'd humour: *unrestrained caprices*
220 contagious: *pestilential*   229 accidents: *events*   234 sullen: *dull*

Scene Three

[*The Same*]

Enter the King, Northumberland, Worcester, Hotspur,
Sir Walter Blunt, and others.

King. My blood hath been too cold and temperate,
Unapt to stir at these indignities,
And you have found me; for accordingly
You tread upon my patience: but, be sure,   4
I will from henceforth rather be myself,
Mighty, and to be fear'd, than my condition,
Which hath been smooth as oil, soft as young down,
And therefore lost that title of respect   8
Which the proud soul ne'er pays but to the proud.
  Wor. Our house, my sovereign liege, little deserves
The scourge of greatness to be us'd on it;
And that same greatness too which our own hands   12
Have holp to make so portly.
  North. My lord,—
  King. Worcester, get thee gone; for I do see
Danger and disobedience in thine eye.   16
O, sir, your presence is too bold and peremptory,
And majesty might never yet endure
The moody frontier of a servant brow.
You have good leave to leave us; when we need
Your use and counsel we shall send for you.   21
                               Exit Worcester.
[*To Northumberland.*] You were about to speak.
  North. Yea, my good lord.
Those prisoners in your highness' name demanded,
Which Harry Percy here at Holmedon took,   ·   24

---

3 found me: *guessed my character*   6 condition: *natural disposition*
3 portly: *stately*
9 moody: *angry*   frontier: *the outworks of a fort,* used figuratively

Were, as he says, not with such strength denied
As is deliver'd to your majesty:
Either envy, therefore, or misprision
Is guilty of this fault and not my son.   28

   Hot. My liege, I did deny no prisoners:
But I remember, when the fight was done,
When I was dry with rage and extreme toil,
Breathless and faint, leaning upon my sword,   32
Came there a certain lord, neat, and trimly dress'd,
Fresh as a bridegroom; and his chin, new reap'd,
Show'd like a stubble-land at harvest-home:
He was perfumed like a milliner,   36
And 'twixt his finger and his thumb he held
A pouncet-box, which ever and anon
He gave his nose and took't away again;
Who therewith angry, when it next came there,   40
Took it in snuff: and still he smil'd and talk'd;
And as the soldiers bore dead bodies by,
He call'd them untaught knaves, unmannerly,
To bring a slovenly unhandsome corpse   44
Betwixt the wind and his nobility.
With many holiday and lady terms
He question'd me; among the rest, demanded
My prisoners in your majesty's behalf.   48
I then all smarting with my wounds being cold,
To be so pester'd with a popinjay,
Out of my grief and my impatience
Answer'd neglectingly, I know not what,   52
He should, or he should not; for he made me mad
To see him shine so brisk and smell so sweet
And talk so like a waiting-gentlewoman

26 deliver'd: *reported*   27 misprision: *misapprehension*
36 milliner; *cf. n.*   38 pouncet-box: *a perforated box for perfumes*
41 in snuff: *as an offence* (with play on the word *snuff*)
46 holiday and lady terms: *choice and ladylike expressions*
50 popinjay: *parrot*   51 grief: *pain*

Of guns, and drums, and wounds,—God save the
   mark!—   56
And telling me the sovereign'st thing on earth
Was parmaceti for an inward bruise;
And that it was great pity, so it was,
This villainous saltpetre should be digg'd   60
Out of the bowels of the harmless earth,
Which many a good tall fellow had destroy'd
So cowardly; and but for these vile guns,
He would himself have been a soldier.   64
This bald unjointed chat of his, my lord,
  answer'd indirectly, as I said;
And I beseech you, let not his report
Come current for an accusation   68
Betwixt my love and your high majesty.
  Blunt. The circumstance consider'd, good my lord,
What e'er Lord Harry Percy then had said
To such a person and in such a place,   72
At such a time, with all the rest re-told,
May reasonably die and never rise
To do him wrong, or any way impeach
What then he said, so he unsay it now.   76
  King. Why, yet he doth deny his prisoners,
But with proviso and exception,
That we at our own charge shall ransom straight
His brother-in-law, the foolish Mortimer;   80
Who, on my soul, hath wilfully betray'd
The lives of those that he did lead to fight
Against that great magician, damn'd Glendower,
Whose daughter, as we hear, the Earl of March

55 God save the mark; *cf. n.*
57 sovereign'st: *of most supreme excellence.*
58 parmaceti: corrupted form of *spermaceti, a substance found in
  whale-oil*
62 tall: *valiant*   75 impeach: *call in question*
80 brother-in-law; *cf. n. on ll. 145-6*   84 Earl of March: *Mortimer*

Hath lately married. Shall our coffers then   8
Be emptied to redeem a traitor home?
Shall we buy treason, and indent with fears,
When they have lost and forfeited themselves?
No, on the barren mountains let him starve;   8
For I shall never hold that man my friend
Whose tongue shall ask me for one penny cost
To ransom home revolted Mortimer.   9

    Hot. Revolted Mortimer!
He never did fall off, my sovereign liege,
But by the chance of war: to prove that true
Needs no more but one tongue for all those wounds,   9
Those mouthed wounds, which valiantly he took,
When on the gentle Severn's sedgy bank,
In single opposition, hand to hand,
He did confound the best part of an hour   100
In changing hardiment with great Glendower.
Three times they breath'd and three times did they
    drink,
Upon agreement, of swift Severn's flood,
Who then, affrighted with their bloody looks,   104
Ran fearfully among the trembling reeds,
And hid his crisp head in the hollow bank
Blood-stained with these valiant combatants.
Never did base and rotten policy   108
Colour her working with such deadly wounds;
Nor never could the noble Mortimer
Receive so many, and all willingly:
Then let him not be slander'd with revolt.   112

    King. Thou dost belie him, Percy, thou dost
    belie him:
He never did encounter with Glendower:

---

87 indent: *bargain*   94 fall off: *desert*   100 confound: *consume*
101 changing hardiment: *exchanging valour*
106 crisp: *curled*, i.e., *rippled*   109 Colour: *disguise*

I tell thee,
He durst as well have met the devil alone　　116
As Owen Glendower for an enemy.
Art thou not asham'd?　But, sirrah, henceforth
Let me not hear you speak of Mortimer:
Send me your prisoners with the speediest means,　120
Or you shall hear in such a kind from me
As will displease you.　My Lord Northumberland,
We license your departure with your son.
Send us your prisoners, or you will hear of it.　　124

Exit King [with Blunt and train].

Hot. An if the devil come and roar for them,
I will not send them: I will after straight
And tell him so; for I will ease my heart,
Albeit I make a hazard of my head.　　128

North. What! drunk with choler? stay, and pause
　　awhile:
Here comes your uncle.

Enter Worcester.

Hot.　　　　　　　　Speak of Mortimer!
'Zounds! I will speak of him; and let my soul
Want mercy if I do not join with him:　　132
In his behalf I'll empty all these veins,
And shed my dear blood drop by drop i' the dust,
But I will lift the down-trod Mortimer
As high i' the air as this unthankful king,　　136
As this ingrate and canker'd Bolingbroke.

North. Brother, the king hath made your nephew
　　mad.

Wor. Who struck this heat up after I was gone?

Hot. He will, forsooth, have all my prisoners;

---

121 kind: *way*　　125 An if: *even if*　　126 straight: *immediately*
128 Albeit . . . hazard: *though at the risk*
129 choler: *anger*　　137 canker'd: *malignant*　　Bolingbroke; *cf. n.*

And when I urg'd the ransom once again   141
Of my wife's brother, then his cheek look'd pale,
And on my face he turn'd an eye of death,
Trembling even at the name of Mortimer.   144
    Wor. I cannot blame him: was he not proclaim'd
By Richard that dead is the next of blood?
    North. He was; I heard the proclamation:
And then it was when the unhappy king,—   148
Whose wrongs in us God pardon!—did set forth
Upon his Irish expedition;
From whence he, intercepted, did return
To be depos'd, and shortly murdered.   152
    Wor. And for whose death we in the world's wide
        mouth
Live scandaliz'd and foully spoken of.
    Hot. But, soft! I pray you, did King Richard then
Proclaim my brother Edmund Mortimer   156
Heir to the crown?
    North.   He did; myself did hear it.
    Hot. Nay, then I cannot blame his cousin king,
That wish'd him on the barren mountains starve.
But shall it be that you, that set the crown   160
Upon the head of this forgetful man,
And for his sake wear the detested blot
Of murd'rous subornation, shall it be,
That you a world of curses undergo,   164
Being the agents, or base second means,
The cords, the ladder, or the hangman rather?
O! pardon me that I descend so low,
To show the line and the predicament   168
Wherein you range under this subtle king.

145-146 *Cf. n.*   149 in us: *at our hands*
163 murd'rous subornation: *secret prompting to murder*
168 line: *rank*   predicament: *situation, classification*
169 range: *stand*

Shall it for shame be spoken in these days,
Or fill up chronicles in time to come,
That men of your nobility and power,   172
Did gage them both in an unjust behalf,
As both of you—God pardon it!—have done,
To put down Richard, that sweet lovely rose,
And plant this thorn, this canker, Bolingbroke?
And shall it in more shame be further spoken,
That you are fool'd, discarded, and shook off
By him for whom these shames ye underwent?
No; yet time serves wherein you may redeem   180
Your banish'd honours, and restore yourselves
Into the good thoughts of the world again;
Revenge the jeering and disdain'd contempt
Of this proud king, who studies day and night
To answer all the debt he owes to you,   185
Even with the bloody payment of your deaths.
Therefore, I say,—

 Wor.   Peace, cousin! say no more:
And now I will unclasp a secret book,   188
And to your quick-conceiving discontents
I'll read you matter deep and dangerous,
As full of peril and adventurous spirit
As to o'er-walk a current roaring loud,   192
On the unsteadfast footing of a spear.

 Hot. If he fall in, good night! or sink or swim:
Send danger from the east unto the west,
So honour cross it from the north to south,   196
And let them grapple: O! the blood more stirs
To rouse a lion than to start a hare.

 North. Imagination of some great exploit
Drives him beyond the bounds of patience.   200

173 gage them: *pledge themselves*
176 canker: *dog-rose*
        183 disdain'd: *disdainful*

Hot. By heaven methinks it were an easy leap
To pluck bright honour from the pale-fac'd moon,
Or dive into the bottom of the deep,
Where fathom-line could never touch the ground,   204
And pluck up drowned honour by the locks;
So he that doth redeem her thence might wear
Without corrival all her dignities:
But out upon this half-fac'd fellowship!   208

Wor. He apprehends a world of figures here,
But not the form of what he should attend.
Good cousin, give me audience for a while.

Hot. I cry you mercy.

Wor.   Those same noble Scots   212
That are your prisoners,——

Hot.   I'll keep them all;
By God, he shall not have a Scot of them:
No, if a Scot would save his soul, he shall not:
I'll keep them, by this hand.

Wor.   You start away,   216
And lend no ear unto my purposes.
Those prisoners you shall keep.

Hot.   Nay, I will; that's flat:
He said he would not ransom Mortimer;
Forbade my tongue to speak of Mortimer;   220
But I will find him when he lies asleep,
And in his ear I'll holla 'Mortimer!'
Nay,
I'll have a starling shall be taught to speak   224
Nothing but 'Mortimer,' and give it him,
To keep his anger still in motion.

Wor. Hear you, cousin; a word.

207 corrival: *rival*   208 half-fac'd: *half and half*
209 apprehends: *imagines*   figures: *unpractical fancies*
212 cry you mercy: *beg your pardon*
224 starling: *a bird with remarkable powers of mimicry*

Hot. All studies here I solemnly defy,   228
Save how to gall and pinch this Bolingbroke:
And that same sword-and-buckler Prince of Wales,
But that I think his father loves him not,
And would be glad he met with some mischance,
would have him poison'd with a pot of ale.   233
Wor. Farewell, kinsman: I will talk to you
When you are better temper'd to attend.
   North. Why, what a wasp-stung and impatient
      fool   236
Art thou to break into this woman's mood,
Tying thine ear to no tongue but thine own!
   Hot. Why, look you, I am whipp'd and scourg'd
      with rods,
Nettled, and stung with pismires, when I hear
Of this vile politician, Bolingbroke.   241
In Richard's time,—what do ye call the place?—
A plague upon 't—it is in Gloucestershire;—
Twas where the madcap duke his uncle kept,
His uncle York; where I first bow'd my knee
Into this king of smiles, this Bolingbroke,
Sblood!
When you and he came back from Ravenspurgh.
   North. At Berkeley Castle.   249
   Hot. You say true.
Why, what a candy deal of courtesy
This fawning greyhound then did proffer me!
Look, 'when his infant fortune came to age,'   253
And 'gentle Harry Percy,' and 'kind cousin.'
O! the devil take such cozeners.   God forgive me!
Good uncle, tell your tale, for I have done.   256

228 defy: *renounce*
230 sword and buckler: *arms carried by the lower classes; hence,*
   ruffianly
240 pismires: *ants*   244 kept: *lived*   245 York; *cf. n.*
251 candy deal: *sugary lot*   255 cozeners: *swindlers*

Wor. Nay, if you have not, to 't again;
We'll stay your leisure.
    Hot.   I have done, i' faith.
    Wor. Then once more to your Scottish prisoners,
Deliver them up without their ransom straight,
And make the Douglas' son your only mean   261
For powers in Scotland; which, for divers reasons
Which I shall send you written, be assur'd,
Will easily be granted. [*To Northumberland.*] You,
      my lord,   264
Your son in Scotland being thus employ'd,
Shall secretly into the bosom creep
Of that same noble prelate well belov'd,
The Archbishop.   268
    Hot. Of York, is it not?
    Wor. True; who bears hard
His brother's death at Bristol, the Lord Scroop.
I speak not this in estimation,   272
As what I think might be, but what I know
Is ruminated, plotted and set down;
And only stays but to behold the face
Of that occasion that shall bring it on.   276
    Hot. I smell it.
Upon my life it will do wondrous well.
    North. Before the game's afoot thou still lett'st
      slip.
    Hot. Why, it cannot choose but be a noble plot: 280
And then the power of Scotland and of York,
To join with Mortimer, ha?
    Wor.   And so they shall.
    Hot. In faith, it is exceedingly well aim'd.
    Wor. And 'tis no little reason bids us speed,

258 stay: *await*   271 Scroop; *cf. n.*   272 estimation: *conjecture*
279 still: *always*   lett'st slip: *art letting the hounds loose from the*
    leash

'o save our heads by raising of a head;   .   285
'or, bear ourselves as even as we can,
'he king will always think him in our debt,
ınd think we think ourselves unsatisfied,   288
'ill he hath found a time to pay us home.
ınd see already how he doth begin
'o make us strangers to his looks of love.
  Hot. He does, he does: we'll be reveng'd on
    him.   292
  Wor. Cousin, farewell: no further go in this,
'han I by letters shall direct your course.
Vhen time is ripe,—which will be suddenly,—
'll steal to Glendower and Lord Mortimer;   296
Vhere you and Douglas and our powers at once,—
ıs I will fashion it,—shall happily meet,
'o bear our fortunes in our own strong arms,
Vhich now we hold at much uncertainty.   300
  North. Farewell, good brother: we shall thrive, I
    trust.
  Hot. Uncle, adieu: O! let the hours be short,
'ill fields and blows and groans applaud our sport!
                               Exeunt.

ACT SECOND

Scene One

[*Rochester.   An Inn-Yard*]

Enter a Carrier, with a lantern in his hand.

  First Car. Heigh-ho! An 't be not four by
the day I'll be hanged: Charles' Wain is over
the new chimney, and yet our horse not packed.
What, ostler!   4

85 head: *army*   286 even: *prudently*   293 cousin: *kinsman*
`8 happily: *perchance, if all goes well*   2 Charles' Wain; *cf. n.*

Ost. [*within.*] Anon, anon.

First Car. I prithee, Tom, beat Cut's saddle,
put a few flocks in the point: the poor jade is
wrung in the withers out of all cess.   8

Enter another Carrier.

Sec. Car. Peas and beans are as dank here as
a dog, and that is the next way to give poor
jades the bots; this house is turned upside down
since Robin Ostler died.   12

First Car. Poor fellow! never joyed since the
price of oats rose; it was the death of him.

Sec. Car. I think this be the most villainous
house in all London road for fleas: I am stung
like a tench.   17

First Car. Like a tench! by the mass, there
is ne'er a king christen could be better bit than
I have been since the first cock.   20

Sec. Car. Why, they will allow us ne'er a
jordan, and then we leak in the chimney; and
your chamber-lie breeds fleas like a loach.

First Car. What, ostler! come away and be
hanged, come away.   25

Sec. Car. I have a gammon of bacon and
two razes of ginger, to be delivered as far as
Charing-cross.   28

First Car. Godsbody! the turkeys in my
pannier are quite starved. What, ostler! A
plague on thee! hast thou never an eye in thy

6 Cut: *slang name for a horse with a docked tail*
7 flocks: *tufts of wool*   point: *head of the saddle*
8 wrung: *galled*   withers: *neck*   out of all cess: *beyond all reckoning*
9 dank: *mouldy*   10 next: *most direct, surest*
11 bots: *disease of horses caused by worms*   17 tench; *cf. n.*
19 king christen: *Christian king*   22 jordan: *chamber-pot*
23 chamber-lie: *urine*   loach: *a fish that breeds several times a year*
27 razes: *roots*   28 Charing-cross; *cf. n.*

head? canst not hear? An 'twere not as good a deed as drink to break the pate on thee, I am a very villain. Come, and be hanged! hast no faith in thee?

Enter Gadshill.

Gads. Good morrow, carriers. What's o'clock?

First Car. I think it be two o'clock.   37

Gads. I prithee, lend me thy lantern, to see my gelding in the stable.

First Car. Nay, by God, soft: I know a trick worth two of that, i' faith.   41

Gads. I prithee, lend me thine.

Sec. Car. Ay, when? canst tell? Lend me thy lantern, quoth a'? marry, I'll see thee hanged first.   45

Gads. Sirrah carrier, what time do you mean to come to London?

Sec. Car. Time enough to go to bed with a candle, I warrant thee. Come, neighbour Mugs, we'll call up the gentlemen: they will along with company, for they have great charge.

Exeunt [Carriers]. Enter Chamberlain.

Gads. What, ho! chamberlain!   52

Cham. 'At hand, quoth pick-purse.'

Gads. That's even as fair as, 'at hand, quoth the chamberlain'; for thou variest no more from picking of purses than giving direction doth from labouring; thou layest the plot how.   57

Cham. Good morrow, Master Gadshill. It holds current that I told you yesternight: there's a franklin in the wild of Kent hath brought

---

51, charge: *baggage*   52 chamberlain: *servant in charge of chambers*
59 holds current: *proves true*
60 franklin: *freeholder*   wild: *weald, uncultivated country*

three hundred marks with him in gold: I heard
him tell it to one of his company last night at
supper; a kind of auditor; one that hath abun-
dance of charge too, God knows what. They are
up already and call for eggs and butter: they
will away presently.

Gads. Sirrah, if they meet not with Saint
Nicholas' clerks, I'll give thee this neck.   68

Cham. No, I'll none of it: I prithee, keep
that for the hangman; for I know thou worship'st Saint Nicholas as truly as a man of
falsehood may.   72

Gads. What talkest thou to me of the
hangman? If I hang I'll make a fat pair of
gallows; for if I hang, old Sir John hangs with
me, and thou knowest he's no starveling. Tut!
there are other Troyans that thou dreamest not
of, the which for sport sake are content to do
the profession some grace; that would, if matters
should be looked into, for their own credit sake
make all whole. I am joined with no foot-land-
rakers, no long-staff sixpenny strikers, none of
these mad mustachio-purple-hued malt worms;
but with nobility and tranquillity, burgomasters
and great oneyers, such as can hold in, such as
will strike sooner than speak, and speak sooner
than drink, and drink sooner than pray: and
yet I lie; for they pray continually to their
saint, the commonwealth; or, rather, not pray
to her, but prey on her, for they ride up and
down on her and make her their boots.

---

61 mark: *13s. 4d., about $3.35*   67 St. Nicholas' clerks: *thieves; cf. n.*
77 Troyans: *a cant name for rioters and thieves*
81 foot-land-rakers, *etc.; cf. n.*   91 boots: *booty*

Cham. What! the commonwealth their boots? will she hold out water in foul way?   93

Gads. She will, she will; justice hath liquored her. We steal as in a castle, cock-sure; we have the receipt of fern-seed, we walk invisible.   96

Cham. Nay, by my faith, I think you are more beholding to the night than to fern-seed for your walking invisible.

Gads. Give me thy hand: thou shalt have a share in our purchase, as I am a true man.   101

Cham. Nay, rather let me have it, as you are false thief.

Gads. Go to; *homo* is a common name to all men. Bid the ostler bring my gelding out of the stable. Farewell, you muddy knave.   106

[*Exeunt.*

Scene Two

[*Gadshill. The highway*]

Enter Prince, Poins, and Peto.

Poins. Come, shelter, shelter: I have removed Falstaff's horse, and he frets like a gummed velvet.

Prince. Stand close.   4

Enter Falstaff.

Fal. Poins! Poins, and be hanged! Poins!

Prince. Peace, ye fat-kidneyed rascal! What a brawling dost thou keep!

Fal. Where's Poins, Hal?   8

---

94 liquored; *cf. n.*   95 as in a castle: *in perfect security*
96 receipt of fern-seed; *cf. n.*   98 beholding: *obliged*
101 purchase: *plunder* 3 gummed velvet; *cf. n.*   4 close: *out of sight*

Prince. He is walked up to the top of the hill: I'll go seek him.　　　　　　[*Withdraws.*]

Fal. I am accursed to rob in that thief's company; the rascal hath removed my horse and tied him I know not where. If I travel but four foot by the squire further afoot I shall break my wind. Well, I doubt not but to die a fair death for all this, if I 'scape hanging for killing that rogue. I have forsworn his company hourly any time this two-and-twenty years, and yet I am bewitched with the rogue's company. If the rascal have not given me medicines to make me love him, I'll be hanged: it could not be else: I have drunk medicines. Poins! Hal! a plague upon you both! Bardolph! Peto! I'll starve ere I'll rob a foot further. An 'twere not as good a deed as drink to turn true men and leave these rogues, I am the veriest varlet that ever chewed with a tooth. Eight yards of uneven ground is threescore and ten miles afoot with me, and the stony-hearted villains know it well enough. A plague upon 't when thieves cannot be true one to another!

　　　　　　　　　　　　They whistle.

Whew! A plague upon you all! Give me my horse, you rogues; give me my horse and be hanged.　　　　　　　　　　　　　34

Prince. [*Coming forward.*] Peace, ye fat-guts! lie down: lay thine ear close to the ground, and list if thou canst hear the tread of travellers.　　　　　　　　　　　38

Fal. Have you any levers to lift me up again, being down? 'Sblood! I'll not bear mine own

14 squire: *foot-rule*　　　　　20 medicines: *love potions*

flesh so far afoot again for all the coin in thy
father's exchequer. What a plague mean ye to
colt me thus?

Prince. Thou liest: thou art not colted; thou
art uncolted.   45

Fal. I prithee, good Prince Hal, help me to
my horse, good king's son.

Prince. Out, you rogue! shall I be your ostler?

Fal. Go, hang thyself in thine own heir apparent garters! If I be ta'en I'll peach for this. An
I have not ballads made on you all, and sung to
filthy tunes, let a cup of sack be my poison: when
a jest is so forward, and afoot too! I hate it.   53

  Enter Gadshill [and Bardolph].

Gads. Stand.

Fal. So I do, against my will.

Poins. O! 'tis our setter: I know his voice.
Bardolph, what news?   57

Bard. Case ye, case ye; on with your vizards:
there's money of the king's coming down the
hill; 'tis going to the king's exchequer.   60

Fal. You lie, you rogue; 'tis going to the
king's tavern.

Gads. There's enough to make us all.

Fal. To be hanged.   64

Prince. Sirs, you four shall front them in the
narrow lane; Ned Poins and I will walk lower:
if they 'scape from your encounter then they
light on us.   68

Peto. How many be there of them?

Gads. Some eight or ten.

43 colt: *make a fool of*   50 peach: *turn informer*   53 forward: *bold*
56 setter: *the one who set the match; cf. I. ii. 118*
58 Case ye: *put on your masks*

Fal. 'Zounds! will they not rob us?

Prince. What! a coward, Sir John Paunch?

Fal. Indeed, I am not John of Gaunt, your grandfather; but yet no coward, Hal.   74

Prince. Well, we leave that to the proof.

Poins. Sirrah Jack, thy horse stands behind the hedge: when thou needst him there thou shalt find him. Farewell, and stand fast.

                      [Prince and Poins withdraw.]

Fal. Now cannot I strike him if I should be hanged.   80

Prince. Ned, where are our disguises?

Poins. Here, hard by; stand close.

Fal. Now my masters, happy man be his dole, say I: every man to his business.   85

              Enter Travellers.

First Trav. Come, neighbour; the boy shall lead our horses down the hill; we'll walk afoot awhile, and ease our legs.   88

Thieves. Stand!

Travellers. Jesu bless us!

Fal. Strike; down with them; cut the villains' throats: ah! whoreson caterpillars! bacon-fed knaves! they hate us youth: down with them; fleece them.

Travellers. O! we are undone, both we and ours for ever.   96

Fal. Hang ye, gorbellied knaves, are ye undone? No, ye fat chuffs; I would your store were here! On, bacons, on! What! ye knaves,

---

75 proof: *test*
84 happy man be his dole: *happiness be his portion,* or, *luck be with us*
92 whoreson: *miserable*   97 gorbellied: *fat-paunched*
98 chuffs: *misers*   99 bacons: *rustics*

young men must live. You are grand-jurors
are ye? We'll jure ye, i' faith. 101

Here they rob them and bind them. Exeunt.
Enter the Prince and Poins.

Prince. The thieves have bound the true men.
Now could thou and I rob the thieves and go
merrily to London, it would be argument for a
week, laughter for a month, and a good jest for
ever. 106

Poins. Stand close; I hear them coming.

Enter the thieves again.

Fal. Come, my masters; let us share, and
then to horse before day. An the Prince and
Poins be not two arrant cowards, there's no
equity stirring: there's no more valour in that
Poins than in a wild duck. 112

Prince. Your money!

Poins. Villains!

As they are sharing, the Prince and Poins set
upon them. They all run away; and Fal-
staff, after a blow or two, runs away too,
leaving the booty behind them.

Prince. Got with much ease. Now merrily to horse:
The thieves are scatter'd and possess'd with fear
So strongly that they dare not meet each other;
Each takes his fellow for an officer.
Away, good Ned. Falstaff sweats to death
And lards the lean earth as he walks along: 120
Were 't not for laughing I should pity him.

Poins. How the rogue roar'd! *Exeunt.*

101 jure: a verb of Falstaff's own making
104 argument: *subject for conversation*

Scene Three

[Warkworth Castle]

Enter Hotspur, solus, reading a letter.

"But for mine own part, my lord, I could be
well contented to be there, in respect of the love
I bear your house."
He could be contented; why is he not then?   In
respect of the love he bears our house: he shows
in this he loves his own barn better than he
loves our house.   Let me see some more.
    "The purpose you undertake is dangerous;——"   8
Why, that's certain: 'tis dangerous to take a
cold, to sleep, to drink; but I tell you, my lord
fool, out of this nettle, danger, we pluck this
flower, safety.   12
    "The purpose you undertake is dangerous; the
friends you have named uncertain; the time itself
unsorted; and your whole plot too light for the
counterpoise of so great an opposition."   16
Say you so, say you so?   I say unto you again,
you are a shallow cowardly hind, and you lie.
What a lack-brain is this!   By the Lord, our plot
is a good plot as ever was laid; our friends true
and constant: a good plot, good friends, and full
of expectation; an excellent plot, very good
friends.   What a frosty-spirited rogue is this!
Why, my Lord of York commends the plot and
the general course of the action.   'Zounds! an
I were now by this rascal, I could brain him
with his lady's fan.   Is there not my father, my
uncle, and myself?   Lord Edmund Mortimer, my

1 *Cf. n.*   15 unsorted: *ill-chosen*   18 hind: *servant, slave*

Lord of York, and Owen Glendower? Is there
not besides the Douglas? Have I not all their
letters to meet me in arms by the ninth of the
next month, and are they not some of them set
forward already? What a pagan rascal is this!
an infidel! Ha! you shall see now in very sin-
cerity of fear and cold heart, will he to the king
and lay open all our proceedings. O! I could
divide myself and go to buffets, for moving such
a dish of skim milk with so honourable an
action. Hang him! let him tell the king; we
are prepared. I will set forward to-night.   40

Enter his Lady.

How now, Kate! I must leave you within these two
   hours.

Lady P. O, my good lord! why are you thus alone?
For what offence have I this fortnight been
A banish'd woman from my Harry's bed?   44
Tell me, sweet lord, what is 't that takes from thee
Thy stomach, pleasure, and thy golden sleep?
Why dost thou bend thine eyes upon the earth,
And start so often when thou sitt'st alone?   48
Why hast thou lost the fresh blood in thy cheeks,
And given my treasures and my rights of thee
To thick-eyed musing and curst melancholy?
In thy faint slumbers I by thee have watch'd,   52
And heard thee murmur tales of iron wars,
Speak terms of manage to thy bounding steed,
Cry, 'Courage! to the field!' And thou hast talk'd
Of sallies and retires, of trenches, tents,   56
Of palisadoes, frontiers, parapets,

37 divide myself; *cf. n.*
41 Kate; *cf. n.*   46 stomach: *appetite*   50-51 *Cf. n.*
51 curst: *perverse*   54 manage: *direction*   56 retires: *retreats*
57 palisadoes: *sharp stakes driven into the ground as defence against
   cavalry*   frontiers: *outworks; cf. I. iii. 19*

Of basilisks, of cannon, culverin,
Of prisoners' ransom, and of soldiers slain,
And all the currents of a heady fight.   60
Thy spirit within thee hath been so at war,
And thus hath so bestirr'd thee in thy sleep,
That beads of sweat have stood upon thy brow,
Like bubbles in a late-disturbed stream;   64
And in thy face strange motions have appear'd,
Such as we see when men restrain their breath
On some great sudden hest.   O! what portents are
    these?
Some heavy business hath my lord in hand,   68
And I must know it, else he loves me not.
    Hot. What, ho!   [*Enter Servant.*]   Is Gilliams
      with the packet gone?
    Serv. He is, my lord, an hour ago.
    Hot. Hath Butler brought those horses from the
      sheriff?   72
    Serv. One horse, my lord, he brought even now.
    Hot. What horse? a roan, a crop-ear, is it not?
    Serv. It is, my lord.
    Hot.   That roan shall be my throne.
Well, I will back him straight: O, *Esperance!*
Bid Butler lead him forth into the park.
                 [*Exit Servant.*]
    Lady P. But hear you, my lord.
    Hot. What sayst thou, my lady?
    Lady P. What is it carries you away?   80
    Hot. Why, my horse, my love, my horse.
    Lady P. Out, you mad-headed ape!
A weasel hath not such a deal of spleen
As you are toss'd with.   In faith,   84

58 basilisks; *cf. n.*   60 currents: *occurrences*   heady: *headlong*
67 hest: *command*
76 *Esperance:* the motto of the Percy family   83 spleen: *caprice*

I'll know your business, Harry, that I will.
I fear my brother Mortimer doth stir
About his title, and hath sent for you
To line his enterprise. But if you go—   88
    Hot. So far afoot, I shall be weary love.
    Lady P. Come, come, you paraquito, answer me
Directly unto this question that I ask.
In faith, I'll break thy little finger, Harry,   92
An if thou wilt not tell me all things true.
    Hot. Away,
Away, you trifler! Love! I love thee not,
I care not for thee, Kate: this is no world   96
To play with mammets and to tilt with lips:
We must have bloody noses and crack'd crowns,
And pass them current too. God's me, my horse!
What sayst thou, Kate? what wouldst thou have
        with me?   100
    Lady P. Do you not love me? do you not, indeed?
Well, do not, then; for since you love me not,
I will not love myself. Do you not love me?
Nay, tell me if you speak in jest or no.   104
    Hot. Come, wilt thou see me ride?
And when I am o' horseback, I will swear
I love thee infinitely. But hark you, Kate;
I must not have you henceforth question me   108
Whither I go, nor reason whereabout.
Whither I must, I must; and, to conclude,
This evening must I leave you, gentle Kate.
I know you wise; but yet no further wise   112
Than Harry Percy's wife: constant you are,
But yet a woman: and for secrecy,
No lady closer; for I well believe
Thou wilt not utter what thou dost not know;

88 line: *strengthen*   97 mammets: *dolls*   98 crack'd crowns; *cf. n.*

And so far will I trust thee, gentle Kate.   117
  Lady P. How! so far?
  Hot. Not an inch further. But, hark you, Kate;
Whither I go, thither shall you go too;   120
To-day will I set forth, to-morrow you.
Will this content you, Kate?
  Lady P.   It must, of force. *'*
                                       Exeunt.

Scene Four

[Eastcheap. The Boar's Head Tavern]
Enter Prince and Poins.

  Prince. Ned, prithee, come out of that fat
room, and lend me thy hand to laugh a little.
  Poins. Where hast been, Hal?   3
  Prince. With three or four loggerheads a-
mongst three or four score hogsheads. I have
sounded the very base string of humility. Sirrah, I am sworn brother to a leash of drawers,
and can call them all by their christen names,
as Tom, Dick, and Francis. They take it already
upon their salvation, that though I be but Prince
of Wales, yet I am the king of courtesy; and tell
me flatly I am no proud Jack, like Falstaff, but
a Corinthian, a lad of mettle, a good boy,—by
the Lord, so they call me,—and when I am king
of England, I shall command all the good lads
in Eastcheap. They call drinking deep, dyeing
scarlet; and when you breathe in your watering,
they cry 'hem!' and bid you play it off. To

1 fat room: *room containing vats* (?), or *close, stuffy room*
7 leash: *three on a string*   drawers: *waiters*
9 take it . . . upon: *swear by*   13 Corinthian: *good sport*
17 breathe . . . watering: *stop to breathe while drinking*
18 play: *toss*

conclude, I am so good a proficient in one
quarter of an hour, that I can drink with any
tinker in his own language during my life. I
tell thee, Ned, thou hast lost much honour that
thou wert not with me in this action. But, sweet
Ned,—to sweeten which name of Ned, I give thee
this pennyworth of sugar, clapped even now into
my hand by an underskinker, one that never
spake other English in his life than—'Eight
shillings and sixpence,' and—'You are welcome,'
with this shrill addition,—'Anon, anon, sir!
Score a pint of bastard in the Half-moon,' or
so. But, Ned, to drive away the time till Falstaff
come, I prithee do thou stand in some by-room,
while I question my puny drawer to what end
he gave me the sugar; and do thou never leave
calling 'Francis!' that his tale to me may be
nothing but 'Anon.' Step aside, and I'll show
thee a precedent.　　　　　　　　　　　37

　Poins. Francis!
　Prince. Thou art perfect.
　Poins. Francis!　　　　　　　　*[Exit Poins.]*

　　　　Enter Drawer [Francis].

　Fran. Anon, anon, sir. Look down into the
Pomgarnet, Ralph.
　Prince. Come hither, Francis.
　Fran. My lord.　　　　　　　　　　　44
　Prince. How long hast thou to serve, Francis?
　Fran. Forsooth, five years, and as much as to—
　Poins [within.] Francis!

21 tinker; *cf. n.*　　　　　　26 underskinker: *under-tapster*
30 bastard: *sweet Spanish wine*　　Half-moon: *name of a room in the*
　inn　　　　　　　　　　　　　*inn*
37 precedent: *example*
42 Pomgarnet: *'Pomegranate'; a room in the inn*

Fran. Anon, anon, sir.   48

Prince. Five years! by'r lady a long lease for
the clinking of pewter. But, Francis, darest
thou be so valiant as to play the coward with
thy indenture and show it a fair pair of heels
and run from it?   53

Fran. O Lord, sir! I'll be sworn upon all the
books in England, I could find in my heart—

Poins [*within.*] Francis!   56

Fran. Anon, sir.

Prince. How old art thou, Francis?

Fran. Let me see—about Michaelmas next I
shall be—   60

Poins [*within.*] Francis!

Fran. Anon, sir. Pray you, stay a little, my
lord.

Prince. Nay, but hark you, Francis. For the
sugar thou gavest me, 'twas a pennyworth,
was 't not?   66

Fran. O Lord, sir! I would it had been two.

Prince. I will give thee for it a thousand
pound: ask me when thou wilt and thou shalt
have it.

Poins [*within.*] Francis!

Fran. Anon, anon.   72

Prince. Anon, Francis? No, Francis; but
to-morrow, Francis; or, Francis, o' Thursday; or, indeed, Francis, when thou wilt. But,
Francis!   76

Fran. My lord?

Prince. Wilt thou rob this leathern-jerkin,
crystal-button, not-pated, agate-ring, puke-

59 Michaelmas; *cf. n.*
79 not-pated: *nut-pated,* i.e., *closely cropped head*   puke: *fine wool*

stocking, caddis-garter, smooth-tongue, Spanish-
pouch,— 81

Fran. O Lord, sir, who do you mean?

Prince. Why then, your brown bastard is
your only drink; for, look you, Francis, your
white canvas doublet will sully. In Barbary, sir,
it cannot come to so much.

Fran. What, sir?

Poins [*within.*] Francis! 88

Prince. Away, you rogue! Dost thou not
hear them call?

Here they both call him; the Drawer stands
amazed, not knowing which way to go.

Enter Vintner.

Vint. What! standest thou still, and hearest
such a calling? Look to the guests within.
[*Exit Drawer.*] My lord, old Sir John, with
half a dozen more, are at the door: shall I let
them in?

Prince. Let them alone awhile, and then
open the door. [*Exit Vintner.*] Poins! 97

Enter Poins.

Poins. Anon, anon, sir.

Prince. Sirrah, Falstaff and the rest of the
thieves are at the door: shall we be merry? 100

Poins. As merry as crickets, my lad. But
hark ye; what cunning match have you made
with this jest of the drawer? come, what's the
issue? 104

Prince. I am now of all humours that have

---

80 caddis: *worsted ribbon*
reproach
83 ff.; *cf. n.*

Spanish-pouch: *an indefinite term of*
reproach

102 match: *bargain*

show'd themselves humours since the old days
of goodman Adam to the pupil age of this
present twelve o'clock at midnight. [*Drawer
crosses the stage, with bottles.*] What's o'clock,
Francis?   110

Fran. Anon, anon, sir.   [*Exit.*]

Prince. That ever this fellow should have
fewer words than a parrot, and yet the son of a
woman! His industry is up-stairs and down-
stairs; his eloquence the parcel of a reckoning.
I am not yet of Percy's mind, the Hotspur of the
North; he that kills me some six or seven dozen
of Scots at a breakfast, washes his hands, and
says to his wife, 'Fie upon this quiet life! I
want work.' 'O my sweet Harry,' says she, 'how
many hast thou killed to-day?' 'Give my roan
horse a drench,' says he, and answers, 'Some
fourteen,' an hour after, 'a trifle, a trifle.' I
prithee call in Falstaff: I'll play Percy, and that
damned brawn shall play Dame Mortimer his
wife. 'Rivo!' says the drunkard. Call in ribs,
call in tallow.   127

*Enter Falstaff, [Bardolph, Peto, and Gadshill. The
Drawer follows, with wine.]*

Poins. Welcome, Jack: where hast thou been?
Fal. A plague of all cowards, I say, and a
vengeance too! marry, and amen! Give me a
cup of sack, boy. Ere I lead this life long,
I'll sew nether-stocks and mend them and foot
them too. A plague of all cowards! Give me a

107 pupil age: *youthful time*
115 parcel of a reckoning: *an item on a bill*
122 drench: *bran and water*   125 brawn; *cf. n.*
126 'Rivo': *a Spanish* (?) *exclamation of drunkards*
132 nether-stocks: *short stockings*

cup of sack, rogue.—Is there no virtue extant?

He drinketh.

Prince. Didst thou never see Titan kiss a dish
of butter—pitiful-hearted Titan—that melted at
the sweet tale of the sun? if thou didst, then
behold that compound. 138

Fal. You rogue, here's lime in this sack too:
there is nothing but roguery to be found in
villainous man: yet a coward is worse than a cup
of sack with lime in it, a villainous coward! Go
thy ways, old Jack; die when thou wilt. If manhood, good manhood, be not forgot upon the
face of the earth, then am I a shotten herring.
There live not three good men unhanged in
England, and one of them is fat and grows old:
God help the while! a bad world, I say. I would
I were a weaver; I could sing psalms or anything. A plague of all cowards, I say still.

Prince. How now, wool-sack! what mutter
you? 152

Fal. A king's son! If I do not beat thee out
of thy kingdom with a dagger of lath, and drive
all thy subjects afore thee like a flock of wild
geese, I'll never wear hair on my face more.
You Prince of Wales! 157

Prince. Why, you whoreson round man,
what's the matter?

Fal. Are you not a coward? answer me to
that; and Poins there? 161

Poins. 'Zounds! ye fat paunch, an ye call
me coward, by the Lord, I'll stab thee.

Fal. I call thee coward! I'll see thee damned

---

134 virtue: *courage*   135 Titan, *etc.; cf. n.*
145 shotten herring: *a herring that has cast its roe*   149 weaver; *cf. n.*

ere I call thee coward; but I would give a thousand pound I could run as fast as thou canst.
You are straight enough in the shoulders; you
care not who sees your back: call you that back-
ing of your friends? A plague upon such back-
ing! give me them that will face me. Give me
a cup of sack: I am a rogue if I drunk to-
day.   172

   Prince. O villain! thy lips are scarce wiped
since thou drunkest last.

   Fal. All's one for that.   *He drinketh.*
A plague of all cowards, still say I.   176

   Prince. What's the matter?

   Fal. What's the matter? there be four of us
here have ta'en a thousand pound this day
morning.   180

   Prince. Where is it, Jack? where is it?

   Fal. Where is it! taken from us it is: a hundred upon poor four of us.

   Prince. What, a hundred, man?   184

   Fal. I am a rogue, if I were not at half-sword
with a dozen of them two hours together. I
have 'scap'd by miracle. I am eight times thrust
through the doublet, four through the hose;
my buckler cut through and through; my sword
hacked like a hand-saw: *ecce signum!* I never
dealt better since I was a man: all would not
do. A plague of all cowards! Let them speak:
if they speak more or less than truth, they are
villains and the sons of darkness.

   Prince. Speak, sirs; how was it?

   Gads. We four set upon some dozen,—   196

   Fal. Sixteen, at least, my lord.

185 at half-sword: *at close quarters* 190 *ecce signum:* behold the proof

Gads. And bound them.

Peto. No, no, they were not bound.

Fal. You rogue, they were bound, every man of them; or I am a Jew else, an Ebrew Jew.

Gads. As we were sharing, some six or seven fresh men set upon us,—   204

Fal. And unbound the rest, and then come in the other.

Prince. What, fought ye with them all?

Fal. All! I know not what ye call all; but if I fought not with fifty of them, I am a bunch of radish: if there were not two or three and fifty upon poor old Jack, then am I no two-legged creature.   212

Prince. Pray God you have not murdered some of them.

Fal. Nay, that's past praying for: I have peppered two of them: two I am sure I have paid, two rogues in buckram suits. I tell thee what, Hal, if I tell thee a lie, spit in my face, call me horse. Thou knowest my old ward; here I lay, and thus I bore my point. Four rogues in buckram let drive at me,—   221

Prince. What, four? thou saidst but two even now.

Fal. Four, Hal; I told thee four.   224

Poins. Ay, ay, he said four.

Fal. These four came all a-front, and mainly thrust at me. I made me no more ado but took all their seven points in my target, thus.   228

217 paid: *killed*
226 mainly: *strongly (cf. might and main)*   228 target: *shield*

Prince. Seven? why, there were but four even now.

Fal. In buckram?

Poins. Ay, four, in buckram suits.   232

Fal. Seven, by these hilts, or I am a villain else.

Prince. Prithee, let him alone; we shall have more anon.   236

Fal. Dost thou hear me, Hal?

Prince. Ay, and mark thee too, Jack.

Fal. Do so, for it is worth the listening to. These nine in buckram that I told thee of,—   240

Prince. So, two more already.

Fal. Their points being broken,—

Poins. Down fell their hose.

Fal. Began to give me ground; but I followed me close, came in foot and hand, and with a thought seven of the eleven I paid.

Prince. O monstrous! eleven buckram men grown out of two.   248

Fal. But, as the devil would have it, three misbegotten knaves in Kendal-green came at my back and let drive at me; for it was so dark, Hal, that thou couldst not see thy hand.   252

Prince. These lies are like the father that begets them; gross as a mountain, open, palpable. Why, thou clay-brained guts, thou knotty-pated fool, thou whoreson, obscene, greasy tallow-ketch,—   257

Fal. What, art thou mad? art thou mad? is not the truth the truth?

Prince. Why, how couldst thou know these

---

242 points; *cf. n.*   250 Kendal-green; *cf. n.*
255 knotty-pated: *thick-headed*   256 tallow-ketch: *tub of tallow*

men in Kendal-green, when it was so dark thou
couldst not see thy hand? come, tell us your
reason: what sayest thou to this?   263

Poins. Come, your reason, Jack, your reason.

Fal. What, upon compulsion? 'Zounds! an
I were at the strappado, or all the racks in the
world, I would not tell you on compulsion. Give
you a reason on compulsion! if reasons were as
plenty as blackberries I would give no man a
reason upon compulsion, I.   270

Prince. I'll be no longer guilty of this sin:
this sanguine coward, this bed-presser, this
horseback-breaker, this huge hill of flesh;—   273

Fal. 'Sblood, you starveling, you elf-skin, you
dried neat's-tongue, you bull's pizzle, you stock-
fish! O! for breath to utter what is like thee;
you tailor's yard, you sheath, you bow-case, you
vile standing-tuck,—   278

Prince. Well, breathe awhile, and then to it
again; and when thou hast tired thyself in base
comparisons, hear me speak but this.   281

Poins. Mark, Jack.

Prince. We two saw you four set on four and
you bound them, and were masters of their
wealth. Mark now, how a plain tale shall put
you down. Then did we two set on you four, and,
with a word, out-faced you from your prize, and
have it; yea, and can show it you here in the
house. And, Falstaff, you carried your guts away
as nimbly, with as quick dexterity, and roared
for mercy, and still ran and roared, as ever I

266 strappado; *cf. n.*   268 reasons; *cf. n.*   272 sanguine: *red-faced*
275 neat's-tongue: *ox tongue*   stock-fish: *dried cod*
278 standing-tuck: *small rapier standing on end*
287 out-faced: *frightened*

heard bull-calf. What a slave art thou, to hack
thy sword as thou hast done, and then say it
was in fight! What trick, what device, what
starting-hole canst thou now find out to hide
thee from this open and apparent shame? 296

Poins. Come, let's hear, Jack; what trick
hast thou now?

Fal. By the Lord, I knew ye as well as he
that made ye. Why, hear you, my masters: was
it for me to kill the heir-apparent? Should I turn
upon the true prince? Why, thou knowest I am
as valiant as Hercules; but beware instinct: the
lion will not touch the true prince. Instinct is
a great matter, I was a coward on instinct. I
shall think the better of myself and thee during
my life; I for a valiant lion, and thou for a true
prince. But, by the Lord, lads, I am glad you
have the money. Hostess, clap to the doors:
watch to-night, pray to-morrow. Gallants, lads,
boys, hearts of gold, all the titles of good fellowship come to you! What! shall we be merry?
shall we have a play extempore? 313

Prince. Content; and the argument shall be
thy running away.

Fal. Ah! no more of that, Hal, an thou lovest
me! 317

Enter Hostess.

Host. O Jesu! my lord the prince!

Prince. How now, my lady the hostess! what
sayest thou to me? 320

Host. Marry, my lord, there is a nobleman
of the court at door would speak with you: he
says he comes from your father.

295 starting-hole: *subterfuge* (lit. *hunted animal's shelter*)

Prince. Give him as much as will make him a royal man, and send him back again to my mother.

Fal. What manner of man is he?   326

Host. An old man.

Fal. What doth gravity out of his bed at midnight? Shall I give him his answer?

Prince. Prithee, do, Jack.   330

Fal. Faith, and I'll send him packing.   *Exit.*

Prince. Now, sirs: by'r lady, you fought fair; so did you, Peto; so did you, Bardolph: you are lions too, you ran away upon instinct, you will not touch the true prince; no, fie!

Bard. Faith, I ran when I saw others run.   336

Prince. Faith, tell me now in earnest, how came Falstaff's sword so hacked?

Peto. Why he hacked it with his dagger, and said he would swear truth out of England but he would make you believe it was done in fight, and persuaded us to do the like.   342

Bard. Yea, and to tickle our noses with spear-grass to make them bleed, and then to be-slubber our garments with it and swear it' was the blood of true men. I did that I did not this seven year before; I blushed to hear his monstrous devices.   348

Prince. O villain! thou stolest a cup of sack eighteen years ago, and wert taken with the manner, and ever since thou hast blushed ex-tempore. Thou hadst fire and sword on thy side, and yet thou rannest away. What instinct hadst thou for it.

Bard. [*Pointing to his own face.*] My lord, do

you see these meteors? do you behold these
exhalations? 357

Prince. I do.

Bard. What think you they portend?

Prince. Hot livers and cold purses. 360

Bard. Choler, my lord, if rightly taken.

Prince. No, if rightly taken, halter.—

Enter Falstaff.

Here comes lean Jack, here comes bare-bone.—
How now, my sweet creature of bombast! How
long is 't ago, Jack, since thou sawest thine own
knee? 366

Fal. My own knee! When I was about thy
years, Hal, I was not an eagle's talon in the
waist; I could have crept into any alderman's
thumb-ring. A plague of sighing and grief! it
blows a man up like a bladder. There's villainous news abroad: here was Sir John Bracy from
your father: you must to the court in the morning. That same mad fellow of the north, Percy,
and he of Wales, that gave Amaimon the bastinado and made Lucifer cuckold, and swore
the devil his true liegeman upon the cross of a
Welsh hook—what a plague call you him? 378

Poins. O, Glendower.

Fal. Owen, Owen, the same; and his son-in-
law Mortimer; and old Northumberland; and
that sprightly Scot of Scots, Douglas, that runs
o' horseback up a hill perpendicular.

Prince. He that rides at high speed and with
his pistol kills a sparrow flying. 385

357 exhalations: *meteors* 364 bombast: *cotton stuffing*
375 Amaimon: *a devil* bastinado: *a cudgelling*
378 Welsh hook: *weapon resembling a halberd*

Fal. You have hit it.

Prince. So did he never the sparrow.

Fal. Well, that rascal hath good mettle in him; he will not run. 389

Prince. Why, what a rascal art thou then to praise him so for running!

Fal. O' horseback, ye cuckoo! but, afoot he will not budge a foot. 393

Prince. Yes, Jack, upon instinct.

Fal. I grant ye, upon instinct. Well, he is there too, and one Mordake, and a thousand blue-caps more. Worcester is stolen away to-night; thy father's beard is turned white with the news: you may buy land now as cheap as stinking mackerel. 400

Prince. Why then, it is like, if there come a hot June and this civil buffeting hold, we shall buy maidenheads as they buy hob-nails, by the hundreds. 404

Fal. By the mass, lad, thou sayest true; it is like we shall have good trading that way. But tell me, Hal, art thou not horribly afeard? thou being heir apparent, could the world pick thee out three such enemies again as that fiend Douglas, that spirit Percy, and that devil Glendower? Art thou not horribly afraid? doth not thy blood thrill at it? 412

Prince. Not a whit, i' faith; I lack 'some of thy instinct.

Fal. Well, thou wilt be horribly chid to-morrow when thou comest to thy father: if thou love me, practise an answer. 417

397 blue-caps: *Scotchmen (so-called from their blue bonnets)*

Prince. Do thou stand for my father, and examine me upon the particulars of my life.

Fal. Shall I? content: this chair shall be my state, this dagger my sceptre, and this cushion my crown.   422

Prince. Thy state is taken for a joint-stool, thy golden sceptre for a leaden dagger, and thy precious rich crown for a pitiful bald crown! 425

Fal. Well, an the fire of grace be not quite out of thee, now shalt thou be moved. Give me a cup of sack to make mine eyes look red, that it may be thought I have wept; for I must speak in passion, and I will do it in King Cambyses' vein.

Prince. Well, here is my leg.

Fal. And here is my speech. Stand aside, nobility.   434

Host. O Jesu! This is excellent sport, i' faith!

Fal. Weep not, sweet queen, for trickling tears are vain.   436

Host. O, the father! how he holds his countenance.

Fal. For God's sake, lords, convey my tristful queen,

For tears do stop the flood-gates of her eyes. 440

Host. O Jesu! he doth it as like one of these harlotry players as ever I see!

Fal. Peace, good pint-pot! peace, good ticklebrain! [*Bardolph conveys the Hostess from the stage.*] Harry, I do not only marvel where thou spendest thy time, but also how thou art accom-

---

421 state: *throne of state*   430 passion: *sorrow*   Cambyses'; *cf. n.*
432 leg: *bow*   439 tristful: *sorrowful*   442 harlotry: *rascally*
443 tickle-brain: *a strong liquor; cf. n.*   444-467 *Cf. n.*

panied: for though the camomile, the more it is
trodden on the faster it grows, yet youth, the
more it is wasted the sooner it wears: That thou
art my son, I have partly thy mother's word, partly my own opinion; but chiefly, a villainous trick
of thine eye and a foolish hanging of thy nether
lip, that doth warrant me. If then thou be son to
me, here lies the point; why, being son to me,
art thou so pointed at? Shall the blessed sun of
heaven prove a micher and eat blackberries? a
question not to be asked. Shall the son of England prove a thief and take purses? a question
to be asked. There is a thing, Harry, which thou
hast often heard of, and it is known to many in
our land by the name of pitch: this pitch, as ancient writers do report, doth defile; so doth the
company thou keepest; for, Harry, now I do not
speak to thee in drink, but in tears, not in pleasure but in passion, not in words only, but in
woes also. And yet there is a virtuous man
whom I have often noted in thy company, but I
know not his name.   467

Prince. What manner of man, an it like your
majesty?

Fal. A goodly portly man, i' faith, and a cor-
pulent; of a cheerful look, a pleasing eye, and a
most noble carriage; and, as I think, his age
some fifty, or by'r lady, inclining to threescore;
and now I remember me, his name is Falstaff: if
that man should be lewdly given, he deceiveth
me; for, Harry, I see virtue in his looks. If then
the tree may be known by the fruit, as the fruit

446 camomile: *a strong-scented herb*
451 nether: *lower*   455 micher: *truant*

by the tree, then, peremptorily I speak it, there is
virtue in that Falstaff: him keep with, the rest
banish. And tell me now, thou naughty varlet,
tell me, where hast thou been this month?

Prince. Dost thou speak like a king? Do
thou stand for me, and I'll play my father.   483

Fal. Depose me? if thou dost it half so
gravely, so majestically, both in word and
matter, hang me up by the heels for a rabbit-
sucker or a poulter's hare.

Prince. Well, here I am set.   488

Fal. And here I stand. Judge, my masters.

Prince. Now, Harry! whence come you?

Fal. My noble lord, from Eastcheap.

Prince. The complaints I hear of thee are
grievous.   493

Fal. 'Sblood, my lord, they are false!
[*Aside to Prince.*] Nay, I'll tickle ye for a young
prince, i' faith.

Prince. Swearest thou, ungracious boy? henceforth ne'er look on me. Thou art violently carried away from grace: there is a devil haunts
thee in the likeness of an old fat man; a tun of
man is thy companion. Why dost thou con-
verse with that trunk of humours, that bolting-
hutch of beastliness, that swoln parcel of dropsies,
that huge bombard of sack, that stuffed cloak-
bag of guts, that roasted Manningtree ox with
the pudding in his belly, that reverend vice, that
grey iniquity, that father ruffian, that vanity in

486-487 *Cf. n.*   495 *Cf. n.*
501 trunk of humours: *chest full of caprices*   bolting-hutch: *bin for*
      sifting meal
503 bombard: *large leather vessel for holding liquor*   cloak-bag:
      portmanteau
504 Manningtree: *cf. n.*

years? Wherein is he good but to taste sack and
drink it? wherein neat and cleanly but to carve
a capon and eat it? wherein cunning but in
craft? wherein crafty but in villainy? wherein
villainous but in all things? wherein worthy but
in nothing?   512

Fal. I would your Grace would take me with
you: whom means your Grace?

Prince. That villainous abominable misleader
of youth, Falstaff, that old white-bearded Satan.

Fal. My lord, the man I know.   517

Prince. I know thou dost.

Fal. But to say I know more harm in him
than in myself were to say more than I know.
That he is old, the more the pity, his white
hairs do witness it; but that he is, saving your
reverence, a whoremaster, that I utterly deny.
If sack and sugar be a fault, God help the
wicked! If to be old and merry be a sin, then
many an old host that I know is damned: if to
be fat be to be hated, then Pharaoh's lean kine
are to be loved. No, my good lord; banish Peto,
banish Bardolph, banish Poins; but for sweet
Jack Falstaff, kind Jack Falstaff, true Jack Falstaff, valiant Jack Falstaff, and therefore more
valiant, being, as he is, old Jack Falstaff, banish
not him thy Harry's company: banish not him
thy Harry's company: banish plump Jack, and
banish all the world.   535

Prince. I do, I will.

Enter Bardolph, running.

13 take me with you: *let me follow your meaning*
22 saving . . . reverence: *an apologetic phrase introducing a remark
that might offend the hearer*
27 *Cf. n.*

Bard. O! my lord, my lord, the sheriff with a most monstrous watch is at the door.

Fal. Out, ye rogue! Play out the play: I have much to say in the behalf of that Falstaff.

Enter the Hostess.

Host. O Jesu! my lord, my lord!   541

Prince. Heigh, heigh! the devil rides upon a fiddle-stick: what's the matter?

Host. The sheriff and all the watch are at the door: they are come to search the house. Shall I let them in?   546

Fal. Dost thou hear, Hal? never call a true piece of gold a counterfeit. Thou art essentially mad without seeming so.   549

Prince. And thou a natural coward without instinct.

Fal. I deny your major. If you will deny the sheriff, so; if not, let him enter: if I become not a cart as well as another man, a plague on my bringing up! I hope I shall as soon be strangled with a halter as another.   556

Prince. Go, hide thee behind the arras: the rest walk up above. Now, my masters, for a true face and good conscience.

Fal. Both which I have had; but their date is out, and therefore I'll hide me.   *Exit.*   561

Prince. Call in the sheriff.

Enter the Sheriff and the Carrier.

Now, master sheriff, what's your will with me?

547-549 *Cf. n.*   552 major: *major premise*
554 cart: *cart used for taking criminals to the gallows*
557 arras: *hanging screen of tapestry placed around the walls of a room*
557-558 *Cf. n.*

Sher. First, pardon me, my lord. A hue and cry 564
Hath follow'd certain men unto this house.
Prince. What men?
Sher. One of them is well known, my gracious lord,
A gross fat man.
Car. As fat as butter. 568
Prince. The man, I do assure you, is not here,
For I myself at this time have employ'd him.
And, sheriff, I will engage my word to thee,
That I will, by to-morrow dinner-time, 572
Send him to answer thee, or any man,
For anything he shall be charg'd withal:
And so let me entreat you leave the house.
Sher. I will, my lord. There are two gentle-
men 576
Have in this robbery lost three hundred marks.
Prince. It may be so: if he have robb'd these men,
He shall be answerable; and so farewell.
Sher. Good night, my noble lord. 580
Prince. I think it is good morrow, is it not?
Sher. Indeed, my lord, I think it be two o'clock.
Exit [*with Carrier*].
Prince. This oily rascal is known as well as Paul's.
Go, call him forth. 584
Peto. Falstaff! fast asleep behind the arras,
and snorting like a horse.
Prince. Hark, how hard he fetches breath.
Search his pockets.
*He searcheth his pockets, and findeth certain
papers.*
What hast thou found? 590
Peto. Nothing but papers, my lord.

83 Paul's: *St. Paul's Cathedral*

Prince. Let's see what they be: read them.

Peto. "Item, A Capon . . . . 2*s.* 2*d.*
    Item, Sauce . . . . . 4*d.*
    Item, Sack, two gallons . . 5*s.* 8*d.*
    Item, Anchovies and sack after
        supper . . . . . 2*s.* 6*d.*
    Item, Bread . . . . . ob."

Prince. O monstrous! but one half-penny-
worth of bread to this intolerable deal of sack!
What there is else, keep close; we'll read it at
more advantage. There let him sleep till day.
I'll to the court in the morning. We must all to
the wars, and thy place shall be honourable. I'll
procure this fat rogue a charge of foot; and,
I know, his death will be a march of twelve-
score. The money shall be paid back again
with advantage. Be with me betimes in the
morning; and so good morrow, Peto.   608

Peto. Good morrow, good my lord.   *Exeunt.*

ACT THIRD

Scene One

[Bangor.   The Archdeacon's House]

*Enter Hotspur, Worcester, Lord Mortimer,
Owen Glendower.*

Mort. These promises are fair, the parties sure,
And our induction full of prosperous hope.

Hot. Lord Mortimer, and cousin Glendower,
Will you sit down?   4

598 ob.: *obolus* = *half-penny*
604 charge of foot: *command of infantry*
607 advantage: *interest*   2 induction: *beginning*

And uncle Worcester? A plague upon it!
I have forgot the map.
    Glend.   No, here it is.
Sit, cousin Percy; sit, good cousin Hotspur;
For by that name as oft as Lancaster   8
Doth speak of you, his cheek looks pale and with'
A rising sigh he wisheth you in heaven.
    Hot. And you in hell, as often as he hears
Owen Glendower spoke of.   12
    Glend. I cannot blame him: at my nativity
The front of heaven was full of fiery shapes,
Of burning cressets; and at my birth
The frame and huge foundation of the earth   16
Shak'd like a coward.
    Hot. Why, so it would have done at the same
season, if your mother's cat had but kittened,
though yourself had never been born.   20
    Glend. I say the earth did shake when I was born.
    Hot. And I say the earth was not of my mind,
If you suppose as fearing you it shook.
    Glend. The heavens were all on fire, the earth did
    tremble.   24
    Hot. O! then the earth shook to see the heavens
    on fire,
And not in fear of your nativity.
Diseased nature oftentimes breaks forth
In strange eruptions; oft the teeming earth   28
Is with a kind of colic pinch'd and vex'd
By the imprisoning of unruly wind
Within her womb; which, for enlargement striving,
Shakes the old beldam earth, and topples down
Steeples and moss-grown towers. At your birth   33

3 Lancaster: *the King*   15 cressets: *beacon lights*
31 enlargement: *release*   32 beldam: *grandmother*

Our grandam earth, having this distemperature,
In passion shook.
    Glend.   Cousin, of many men
I do not bear these crossings. Give me leave   36
To tell you once again that at my birth
The front of heaven was full of fiery shapes,
The goats ran from the mountains, and the herds
Were strangely clamorous to the frighted fields.
These signs have mark'd me extraordinary;   41
And all the courses of my life do show
I am not in the roll of common men.
Where is he living, clipp'd in with the sea   44
That chides the banks of England, Scotland, Wales,
Which calls me pupil, or hath read to me?
And bring him out that is but woman's son
Can trace me in the tedious ways of art   48
And hold me pace in deep experiments.
    Hot. I think there's no man speaks better Welsh.
I'll to dinner.
    Mort. Peace, cousin Percy! you will make him
        mad.   52
    Glend. I can call spirits from the vasty deep.
    Hot. Why, so can I, or so can any man;
But will they come when you do call for them?
    Glend. Why, I can teach thee, cousin, to com-
        mand   56
The devil.
    Hot. And I can teach thee, coz, to shame the devil
By telling truth: tell truth and shame the devil.
If thou have power to raise him, bring him hither, 60
And I'll be sworn I have power to shame him hence.
O! while you live, tell truth and shame the devil!

35 passion: *pain*   44 clipp'd in with: *surrounded by*
45 chides: *lashes*   46 read to: *instructed*
48 trace: *follow*   art: *magic*

Mort. Come, come;
No more of this unprofitable chat.   64
  Glend. Three times hath Henry Bolingbroke made
   head
Against my power; thrice from the banks of Wye
And sandy-bottom'd Severn have I sent him
Bootless home and weather-beaten back.   68
  Hot. Home without boots, and in foul weather too!
How 'scapes he agues, in the devil's name?
  Glend. Come, here's the map: shall we divide our
   right
According to our threefold order ta'en?   72
  Mort. The archdeacon hath divided it
Into three limits very equally.
England, from Trent and Severn hitherto,
By south and east, is to my part assign'd: 76
All westward, Wales beyond the Severn shore,
And all the fertile land within that bound,
To Owen Glendower: and, dear coz, to you
The remnant northward, lying off from Trent.   80
And our indentures tripartite are drawn,
Which being sealed interchangeably,
A business that this night may execute,
To-morrow, cousin Percy, you and I   84
And my good Lord Worcester will set forth
To meet your father and the Scottish power,
As is appointed us, at Shrewsbury.
My father Glendower is not ready yet,   88
Nor shall we need his help these fourteen days.
Within that space you may have drawn together
Your tenants, friends, and neighbouring gentlemen.

58 bootless: *without advantage; cf. I. i. 29*   75 hitherto: *to this spot*,
31 indentures tripartite: *three copies of the agreement*
32 interchangeably: *each party signing each copy*

Glend. A shorter time shall send me to you,
    lords;   92
And in my conduct shall your ladies come,
From whom you now must steal and take no leave;
For there will be a world of water shed
Upon the parting of your wives and you.   96
   Hot. Methinks my moiety, north from Burton here,
In quantity equals not one of yours:
See how this river comes me cranking in,
And cuts me from the best of all my land   100
A huge half-moon, a monstrous cantle out.
I'll have the current in this place damm'd up,
And here the smug and silver Trent shall run
In a new channel, fair and evenly: 104
It shall not wind with such a deep indent,
To rob me of so rich a bottom here.
   Glend. Not wind! it shall, it must; you see it doth.
   Mort. Yea, but   108
Mark how he bears his course, and runs me up
With like advantage on the other side;
Gelding the opposed continent as much,
As on the other side it takes from you.   112
   Wor. Yea, but a little charge will trench him here,
And on this north side win this cape of land;
And then he runs straight and even.
   Hot. I'll have it so; a little charge will do it.
   Glend. I will not have it alter'd.
   Hot.   Will not you? 117
   Glend. No, nor you shall not.
   Hot.   Who shall say me nay?
   Glend. Why, that will I.

93 conduct: *escort*   97 moiety: *portion*   99 cranking: *winding*
100 the best of all my land; *cf. n.*   101 cantle: *piece*
103 smug: *neat, trim*   106 bottom: *low, rich land*
111 Gelding: *cutting*   opposed continent: *country opposite*
113 charge: *expense*

Hot.   Let me not understand you then:
Speak it in Welsh.   120
   Glend. I can speak English, lord, as well as you,
For I was train'd up in the English court;
Where, being but young, I framed to the harp
Many an English ditty lovely well,   ·   124
And gave the tongue an helpful ornament;
   Hot. A virtue that was never seen in you.
   Hot. Marry, and I'm glad of it with all my heart.
I had rather be a kitten, and cry mew   128
Than one of these same metre ballad-mongers;
I had rather hear a brazen canstick turn'd,
Or a dry wheel grate on the axle-tree;
And that would set my teeth nothing on edge,
Nothing so much as mincing poetry: 133
'Tis like the forc'd gait of a shuffling nag.
   Glend. Come, you shall have Trent turn'd.
   Hot. I do not care: I'll give thrice so much land 136
To any well-deserving friend;
But in the way of bargain, mark you me,
I'll cavil on the ninth part of a hair.
Are the indentures drawn? shall we be gone?
   Glend. The moon shines fair, you may away by
       night: 141
I'll haste the writer and withal
Break with your wives of your departure hence:
I am afraid my daughter will run mad,   144
So much she doteth on her Mortimer.   *Exit.*
   Mort. Fie, cousin Percy! how you cross my father!
   Hot. I cannot choose: sometimes he angers me
With telling me of the moldwarp and the ant,
Of the dreamer Merlin and his prophecies,   149

130 canstick: *candlestick*   133 mincing: *affected*
143 break with: *inform*   148-152 *Cf. n.*

And of a dragon, and a finless fish,
A clip-wing'd griffin, and a moulten raven,
A couching lion, and a ramping cat,   152
And such a deal of skimble-skamble stuff
As puts me from my faith.   I'll tell thee what;
He held me last night at least nine hours
In reckoning up the several devils' names   156
That were his lackeys: I cried 'hum!' and 'well, go to.'
But mark'd him not a word.   O! he's as tedious
As a tired horse, a railing wife;
Worse than a smoky house.   I had rather live
With cheese and garlic in a windmill, far,   161
Than feed on cates and have him talk to me
In any summer-house in Christendom.

    Mort. In faith, he is a worthy gentleman,   164
Exceedingly well read, and profited
In strange concealments, valiant as a lion
And wondrous affable, and as bountiful
As mines of India.   Shall I tell you, cousin?   168
He holds your temper in a high respect,
And curbs himself even of his natural scope
When you do cross his humour; faith, he does.
I warrant you, that man is not alive   172
Might so have tempted him as you have done,
Without the taste of danger and reproof:
But do not use it oft, let me entreat you.

    Wor. In   faith,   my   lord,   you   are   too   wilful-
        blame;   176
And since your coming hither have done enough
To put him quite beside his patience.
You must needs learn, lord, to amend this fault:

153 skimble-skamble: *nonsensical*   162 cates: *dainties*
163 summer-house: *country house*   165 profited: *proficient*
166 concealments: *mysteries*   170 scope: *tendencies*
176 too wilful-blame: *to be blamed for too great wilfulness*

Though   sometimes   it   show   greatness,   courage,
   blood,—   180
And that's the dearest grace it renders you,—
Yet often times it doth present harsh rage,
Defect of manners, want of government,
Pride, haughtiness, opinion, and disdain: 184
The least of which haunting a nobleman
Loseth men's hearts and leaves behind a stain
Upon the beauty of all parts besides,
Beguiling them of commendation.   188

   Hot. Well, I am school'd; good manners be your
     speed!
Here come our wives, and let us take our leave.

     Enter Glendower, with the Ladies.

   Mort. This is the deadly spite that angers me,
My wife can speak no English, I no Welsh.   192
   Glend. My daughter weeps; she will not part with
     you:
She'll be a soldier too: she'll to the wars.
   Mort. Good father, tell her that she and my aunt
     Percy,
Shall follow in your conduct speedily.   196
     Glendower speaks to her in Welsh, and she
          answers him in the same.
   Glend. She's desperate here; a peevish self-
will'd harlotry, one that no persuasion can do
good upon.   *The lady speaks in Welsh.*
   Mort. I   understand   thy   looks: that   pretty
     Welsh   200
Which thou pour'st down from these swelling heavens

---

180 blood: *spirit*   181 dearest: *most valuable*   182 present: *indicate*
183 government: *self-control*   184 opinion: *arrogance*
188 Beguiling: *cheating*   189 be your speed: *bring you good fortune*
195 aunt: *cf. n. on I. iii. 145-146*
198 harlotry: *silly girl*   200-203 *Cf. n.*

I am too perfect in; and, but for shame,
In such a parley would I answer thee.

The lady again in Welsh.

I understand thy kisses and thou mine,   204
And that's a feeling disputation:
But I will never be a truant, love,
Till I have learn'd thy language; for thy tongue
Makes Welsh as sweet as ditties highly penn'd,
Sung by a fair queen in a summer's bower,   209
With ravishing division, to her lute.

Glend. Nay, if you melt, then will she run mad.

The lady speaks again in Welsh.

Mort. O! I am ignorance itself in this.   212

Glend. She bids you
Upon the wanton rushes lay you down
And rest your gentle head upon her lap,
And she will sing the song that pleaseth you,
And on your eye-lids crown the god of sleep,   217
Charming your blood with pleasing heaviness,
Making such difference 'twixt wake and sleep
As is the difference between day and night   220
The hour before the heavenly-harness'd team
Begins his golden progress in the east.

Mort. With all my heart I'll sit and hear her sing:
By that time will our book, I think, be drawn.

Glend. Do so;   225
And those musicians that shall play to you
Hang in the air a thousand leagues from hence,
And straight they shall be here: sit, and attend.   228

Hot. Come, Kate, thou art perfect in lying
down: come, quick, quick, that I may lay my
head in thy lap.

205 disputation: *conversation*
208 highly penn'd: *written in high style*   210 division: *modulation*
214 wanton: *soft, luxurious*   224 book: *indentures*

Lady P. Go, ye giddy goose.   232

The Music plays.

Hot. Now I perceive the devil understands Welsh;
And 'tis no marvel he is so humorous.
By'r lady, he's a good musician.

Lady P. Then should you be nothing but
musical, for you are altogether governed by
humours. Lie still, ye thief, and hear the lady
sing in Welsh.

Hot. I had rather hear Lady, my brach, howl
in Irish.   240

Lady P. Wouldst thou have thy head broken?

Hot. No.

Lady P. Then be still.

Hot. Neither; 'tis a woman's fault.   244

Lady P. Now, God help thee!

Hot. To the Welsh lady's bed.

Lady P. What's that?

Hot. Peace! she sings.   248

Here the lady sings a Welsh song.

Hot. Come, Kate, I'll have your song too.

Lady P. Not mine, in good sooth.

Hot. Not yours, 'in good sooth!' Heart!
you swear like a comfit-maker's wife! Not you
'in good sooth;' and, 'as true as I live;' and,
'as God shall mend me;' and, 'as sure as day:'
And giv'st such sarcenet surety for thy oaths,
As if thou never walk'dst further than Finsbury.   256
Swear me, Kate, like a lady as thou art,
A good mouth-filling oath; and leave 'in sooth,'
And such protest of pepper-gingerbread,
To velvet-guards and Sunday-citizens.   260

234 humorous: *capricious*   240 brach: *a bitch-hound*
252 comfit-maker: *confectioner*   255 sarcenet: *flimsy; cf. n.*
256 Finsbury; *cf. n.*   260 velvet-guards; *cf. n.*

Come, sing.

 Lady P. I will not sing.

 Hot. 'Tis the next way to turn tailor or be
red-breast teacher. An the indentures be drawn,
I'll away within these two hours; and so, come
in when ye will.   *Exit.*

 Glend. Come, come, Lord Mortimer; you are as
 slow

As hot Lord Percy is on fire to go.   268
By this our book is drawn; we will but seal,
And then to horse immediately.

 Mort. With all my heart.   *Exeunt.*

Scene Two

[*London. The Palace*]

Enter the King, Prince of Wales, and others.

 King. Lords, give us leave; the Prince of Wales
 and I
Must have some private conference: but be near at
 hand,
For we shall presently have need of you.

           Exeunt Lords.

I know not whether God will have it so,   4
For some displeasing service I have done,
That, in his secret doom, out of my blood
He'll breed revengement and a scourge for me;
But thou dost in thy passages of life   8
Make me believe that thou art only mark'd
For the hot vengeance and the rod of heaven
To punish my mistreadings. Tell me else,
Could such inordinate and low desires,   12

---

263 tailor; *cf. n.*   264 red-breast teacher: *trainer of singing-birds*
1 give . . . leave: *leave us*   3 presently: *immediately*
5 doom: *judgment* 8 thy passages of life: *the actions of thy life*

Such poor, such bare, such lewd, such mean attempts,
Such barren pleasures, rude society,
As thou art match'd withal and grafted to,
Accompany the greatness of thy blood   16
And hold their level with thy princely heart?
   Prince. So please your majesty, I would I could
Quit all offences with as clear excuse
As well as I am doubtless I can purge.   20
Myself of many I am charg'd withal:
Yet such extenuation let me beg,
As, in reproof of many tales devis'd,
Which oft the ear of greatness needs must hear,
By smiling pick-thanks and base newsmongers,
I may, for some things true, wherein my youth
Hath faulty wander'd and irregular,
Find pardon on my true submission.   28
   King. God pardon thee! yet let me wonder, Harry,
At thy affections, which do hold a wing
Quite from the flight of all thy ancestors.
Thy place in council thou hast rudely lost,   32
Which by thy younger brother is supplied,
And art almost an alien to the hearts
Of all the court and princes of my blood.
The hope and expectation of thy time   36
Is ruin'd, and the soul of every man
Prophetically do forethink thy fall.
Had I so lavish of my presence been,
So common-hackney'd in the eyes of men,   40
So stale and cheap to vulgar company,
Opinion, that did help me to the crown,
Had still kept loyal to possession
And left me in reputeless banishment,   44

19 Quit: *clear myself*   23 reproof: *refutation*   devis'd: *invented*
30 affections: *tastes*   36 time: *age, reign*   42 Opinion: *public opinion*
43 to possession: *to the possessor,* i.e., *King Richard*

A fellow of no mark nor likelihood.
By being seldom seen, I could not stir,
But like a comet I was wonder'd at;
That men would tell their children, 'This is he;'
Others would say, 'Where? which is Bolingbroke?' 49
And then I stole all courtesy from heaven,
And dress'd myself in such humility
That I did pluck allegiance from men's hearts,
Loud shouts and salutations from their mouths,
Even in the presence of the crowned king.
Thus did I keep my person fresh and new;
My presence, like a robe pontifical,   56
Ne'er seen but wonder'd at: and so my state,
Seldom but sumptuous, showed like a feast,
And won by rareness such solemnity.
The skipping king, he ambled up and down   60
With shallow jesters and rash bavin wits,
Soon kindled and soon burnt; carded his state,
Mingled his royalty with capering fools,
Had his great name profaned with their scorns,
And gave his countenance, against his name,   65
To laugh at gibing boys and stand the push
Of every beardless vain comparative;
Grew a companion to the common streets,   68
Enfeoff'd himself to popularity;
That, being daily swallow'd by men's eyes,
They surfeited with honey and began
To loathe the taste of sweetness, whereof a little
More than a little is by much too much.   73
So, when he had occasion to be seen,

50 stole, *etc.; cf. n.*   61 bavin: *brushwood, which soon burns out*
62 carded; *cf. n.*   65 against his name: *contrary to his dignity*
66 stand the push: *withstand the attack*
67 comparative: *one who affects wit; cf. I. ii.* 90
69 Enfeoff'd himself: *gave himself up entirely*   popularity: *low
company*

He was but as the cuckoo is in June,
Heard, not regarded; seen, but with such eyes
As, sick and blunted with community,   77
Afford no extraordinary gaze,
Such as is bent on sun-like majesty
When it shines seldom in admiring eyes;   80
But rather drows'd and hung their eyelids down,
Slept in his face, and render'd such aspect
As cloudy men use to their adversaries,
Being with his presence glutted, gorg'd, and full.
And in that very line, Harry, stand'st thou;   85
For thou hast lost thy princely privilege
With vile participation: not an eye
But is aweary of thy common sight,   88
Save mine, which hath desir'd to see thee more;
Which now doth that I would not have it do,
Make blind itself with foolish tenderness.

    Prince. I shall hereafter, my thrice gracious
       lord, ·   92
Be more myself.

    King.   For all the world,
As thou art to this hour was Richard then
When I from France set foot at Ravenspurgh;
And even as I was then is Percy now.   96
Now, by my sceptre and my soul to boot,
He hath more worthy interest to the state
Than thou the shadow of succession;
For of no right, nor colour like to right,   100
He doth fill fields with harness in the realm,
Turns head against the lion's armed jaws,
And, being no more in debt to years than thou,

77 community: *commonness*   83 cloudy: *sullen*
87 vile participation: *base companionship*
98 interest: *claim*   99 shadow of succession; *cf. n.*
100 colour: *pretext*   101 harness: *armour*

Leads ancient lords and reverend bishops on   104
To bloody battles and to bruising arms.
What never-dying honour hath he got
Against renowned Douglas! whose high deeds,
Whose hot incursions and great name in arms,
Holds from all soldiers chief majority,   109
And military title capital,
Through all the kingdoms that acknowledge Christ.
Thrice hath this Hotspur, Mars in swathling
    clothes,   112
This infant warrior, in his enterprises
Discomfited great Douglas; ta'en him once,
Enlarged him and made a friend of him,
To fill the mouth of deep defiance up   116
And shake the peace and safety of our throne.
And what say you to this? Percy, Northumberland,
The Archbishop's Grace of York, Douglas, Mortimer,
Capitulate against us and are up.   120
But wherefore do I tell these news to thee?
Why, Harry, do I tell thee of my foes,
Which art my near'st and dearest enemy?
Thou that art like enough, through vassal fear,
Base inclination, and the start of spleen,   125
To fight against me under Percy's pay,
To dog his heels, and curtsy at his frowns,
To show how much thou art degenerate.   128
  Prince. Do not think so; you shall not find it so:
And God forgive them, that so much have sway'd
Your majesty's good thoughts away from me!
I will redeem all this on Percy's head,   132
And in the closing of some glorious day
Be bold to tell you that I am your son;

---

109 majority: *pre-eminence*   110 capital: *chief*
115 enlarged: *released*   120 Capitulate: *form a league*
124 vassal: *slavish*   125 start of spleen: *impulse of ill temper*

When I will wear a garment all of blood
And stain my favours in a bloody mask,   136
Which, wash'd away, shall scour my shame with it:
And that shall be the day, whene'er it lights,
That this same child of honour and renown,
This gallant Hotspur, this all-praised knight,   140
And your unthought-of Harry chance to meet.
For every honour sitting on his helm,
Would they were multitudes, and on my head
My shames redoubled! For the time will come
That I shall make this northern youth exchange   145
His glorious deeds for my indignities.
Percy is but my factor, good my lord,
To engross up glorious deeds on my behalf;
And I will call him to so strict account
That he shall render every glory up,   150
Yea, even the slightest worship of his time,
Or I will tear the reckoning from his heart.
This, in the name of God, I promise here:
The which, if he be pleas'd I shall perform,
I do beseech your majesty may salve   155
The long-grown wounds of my intemperance:
If not, the end of life cancels all bands,
And I will die a hundred thousand deaths
Ere break the smallest parcel of this vow.
    King. A hundred thousand rebels die in this: 160
Thou shalt have charge and sovereign trust herein.

                Enter Blunt.

How now, good Blunt! thy looks are full of speed.
    Blunt. So hath the business that I come to speak of.
Lord Mortimer of Scotland hath sent word   164
That Douglas and the English rebels met,

136 favours: *features*   147 factor: *agent*   148 engross up: *collect*
151 worship: *honour*   157 bands: *bonds*

The eleventh of this month at Shrewsbury.
A mighty and a fearful head they are,—
If promises be kept on every hand,—   168
As ever offer'd foul play in a state.

  King. The Earl of Westmoreland set forth to-day,
With him my son, Lord John of Lancaster;
For this advertisement is five days old.   172
On Wednesday next, Harry, you shall set forward;
On Thursday we ourselves will march: our meeting
Is Bridgenorth; and Harry, you shall march
Through Gloucestershire; by which account,   176
Our business valued, some twelve days hence
Our general forces at Bridgenorth shall meet.
Our hands are full of business: let's away;
Advantage feeds him fat while men delay.   180

                                        Exeunt.

                    Scene Three

        [*Eastcheap. The Boar's Head Tavern*]

              Enter Falstaff and Bardolph.

  Fal. Bardolph, am I not fallen away vilely
since this last action? do I not bate? do I not
dwindle? Why, my skin hangs about me like an
old lady's loose gown; I am withered like an old
apple-john. Well, I'll repent, and that suddenly,
while I am in some liking; I shall be out of heart
shortly, and then I shall have no strength to repent. An I have not forgotten what the inside
of a church is made of, I am a peppercorn, a

172 advertisement: *news*   177 valued: *taken into consideration*
2 bate: *fall off, grow thin*
5 apple-john: *an apple that keeps well but becomes very shrivelled*
6 liking: *(good) bodily condition*
9 peppercorn: *the dried berry from which pepper is ground*

brewer's horse: the inside of a church! Company, villainous •company, hath been the spoil of me.   12

Bard. Sir John, you are so fretful, you cannot live long.

Fal. Why, there is it: come, sing me a bawdy song; make me merry. I was as virtuously given as a gentleman need to be; virtuous enough: swore little; diced not—above seven times a week; went to a bawdy-house not above once in a quarter—of an hour; paid money that I borrowed—three or four times; lived well and in good compass; and now I live out of all order, out of all compass.   23

Bard. Why, you are so fat, Sir John, that you must needs be out of all compass, out of all reasonable compass, Sir John.   26

Fal. Do thou amend thy face, and I'll amend my life: thou art our admiral, thou bearest the lantern in the poop, but 'tis in the nose of thee: thou art the Knight of the Burning Lamp.

Bard. Why, Sir John, my face does you no harm.   32

Fal. No, I'll be sworn; I make as good use of it as many a man doth of a Death's head, or a *memento mori:* I never see thy face but I think upon hell-fire and Dives that lived in purple; for there he is in his robes, burning, burning. If thou wert any way given to virtue, I would swear by thy face; my oath should be, 'By this fire, that's God's angel:' but thou art altogether given over, and wert indeed, but for the light in thy face, the son of utter darkness. When thou rannest up Gadshill in the night to catch my horse, if I did not think thou hadst been an *ignis fatuus* or a ball of wildfire, there's no purchase in money. O! thou art a perpetual triumph, an everlasting bonfire-light. Thou hast saved me a thousand marks in links and torches, walking with thee in the night betwixt tavern and tavern: but the sack that thou hast drunk me would have bought me lights as good cheap at the dearest chandler's in Europe. I have maintained that salamander of yours with fire any time this two-and-thirty years; God reward me for it!   55

Bard. 'Sblood, I would my face were in your belly.

Fal. God-a-mercy! so should I be sure to be heart-burned.

Enter Hostess.

How now, Dame Partlet the hen! have you inquired yet who picked my pocket?   61

Host. Why, Sir John, what do you think, Sir John? Do you think I keep thieves in my house? I have searched, I have inquired, so has my husband, man by man, boy by boy, servant by servant: the tithe of a hair was never lost in my house before.   67

Fal. You lie, hostess: Bardolph was shaved and lost many a hair; and I'll be sworn my pocket was picked. Go to, you are a woman; go.

Host. Who, I? No; I defy thee: God's light!

45 *ignis fatuus:* will o' the wisp   48 links: *torches*
51 as good cheap: *at as good a bargain*
53 salamander: *mythical animal supposed to live in fire*
60 Partlet; *cf. n.*

I was never called so in my own house before.   72

Fal. Go to, I know you well enough.

Host. No, Sir John; you do not know me, Sir John: I know you, Sir John: you owe me money, Sir John, and now you pick a quarrel to beguile me of it: I bought you a dozen of shirts to your back.   78

Fal. Dowlas, filthy dowlas: I have given them away to bakers' wives, and they have made bolters of them.   81

Host. Now, as I am true woman, holland of eight shillings an ell. You owe money here besides, Sir John, for your diet and by-drinkings, and money lent you, four-and-twenty pound.   85

Fal. He had his part of it; let him pay.

Host. He! alas! he is poor; he hath nothing.

Fal. How! poor? look upon his face; what call you rich? let them coin his nose, let them coin his cheeks. I'll not pay a denier. What! will you make a younker of me? shall I not take mine ease in mine inn but I shall have my pocket picked? I have lost a seal-ring of my grandfather's worth forty mark.

Host. O Jesu! I have heard the prince tell him, I know not how oft, that that ring was copper.   97

Fal. How! the prince is a Jack, a sneak-cup; 'sblood! an he were here, I would cudgel him like a dog, if he would say so.   100

Enter the Prince and Peto marching. Falstaff meets them, playing on his truncheon like a fife.

---

79 dowlas: *coarse linen*   81 bolters: *sieves*   82 holland: *fine linen*
83 ell: *yard and a quarter*   90 denier: *the tenth part of a penny*
91 younker: *young greenhorn*
98 sneak-cup: *one who shirks his liquor* (?)

Fal. How now, lad! is the wind in that door,
i' faith? must we all march?

Bard. Yea, two and two, Newgate fashion.

Host. My lord, I pray you, hear me.   104

Prince. What sayest thou, Mistress Quickly?
How does thy husband? I love him well, he is
an honest man.

Host. Good my lord, hear me.   108

Fal. Prithee, let her alone, and list to me.

Prince. What sayest thou, Jack?

Fal. The other night I fell asleep here behind
the arras and had my pocket picked: this house
is turned bawdy-house; they pick pockets.   113

Prince. What didst thou lose, Jack?

Fal. Wilt thou believe me, Hal? three or four
bonds of forty pound a-piece, and a seal-ring of
my grandfather's.   117

Prince. A trifle; some eight-penny matter.

Host. So I told him, my lord; and I said I
heard your Grace say so: and, my lord, he speaks
most vilely of you, like a foul-mouthed man as
he is, and said he would cudgel you.   122

Prince. What! he did not?

Host. There's neither faith, truth, nor womanhood in me else.   125

Fal. There's no more faith in thee than in a
stewed prune; nor no more truth in thee than
in a drawn fox; and for womanhood, Maid
Marian may be the deputy's wife of the ward to
thee. Go, you thing, go.

Host. Say, what thing? what thing?

103 Newgate: *a prison*
128 drawn fox: *a fox driven from cover and tricky in his attempts to get back*
128-129 *Cf. n.*

Fal. What thing! why, a thing to thank
God on.   133

Host. I am no thing to thank God on, I
would thou shouldst know it; I am an honest
man's wife; and, setting thy knighthood aside,
thou art a knave to call me so.   137

Fal. Setting thy womanhood aside, thou art
a beast to say otherwise.

Host. Say, what beast, thou knave thou?   140

Fal. What beast! why, an otter.

Prince. An otter, Sir John! why, an otter?

Fal. Why? she's neither fish nor flesh; a
man knows not where to have her.   144

Host. Thou art an unjust man in saying so:
thou or any man knows where to have me, thou
knave thou!

Prince. Thou sayest true, hostess; and he
slanders thee most grossly.   149

Host. So he doth you, my lord; and said this
other day you ought him a thousand pound.

Prince. Sirrah! do I owe you a thousand
pound?   153

Fal. A thousand pound, Hal! a million: thy
love is worth a million; thou owest me thy love.

Host. Nay, my lord, he called you Jack, and
said he would cudgel you.   157

Fal. Did I, Bardolph?

Bard. Indeed, Sir John, you said so.

Fal. Yea; if he said my ring was copper.   160

Prince. I say 'tis copper: darest thou be as
good as thy word now?

Fal. Why, Hal, thou knowest, as thou art

151 ought: *owed*

but man, I dare; but as thou art prince, I fear
thee as I fear the roaring of the lion's whelp. 165

Prince. And why not as the lion?

Fal. The king himself is to be feared as the ,
lion: dost thou think I'll fear thee as I fear thy
father? nay, an I do, I pray God my girdle
break! 170

Prince. O! if it should, how would thy guts
fall about thy knees. But, sirrah, there's no
room for faith, truth, or honesty in this bosom
of thine; it is all filled up with guts and midriff.
Charge an honest woman with picking thy pocket!
Why, thou whoreson, impudent, embossed rascal,
if there were any thing in thy pocket but tavern
reckonings, memorandums of bawdy-houses, and
one poor pennyworth of sugar-candy to make
thee long-winded; if thy pocket were enriched
with any other injuries but these, I am a villain.
And yet you will stand to it, you will not pocket
up wrong. Art thou not ashamed? 183

Fal. Dost thou hear, Hal? thou knowest in
the state of innocency Adam fell; and what
should poor Jack Falstaff do in the days of
villainy? Thou seest I have more flesh than
another man, and therefore more frailty. You
confess then, you picked my pocket? 189

Prince. It appears so by the story.

Fal. Hostess, I·forgive thee. Go make ready
breakfast; love thy husband, look to thy servants,
cherish thy guests: thou shalt find me tractable
to any honest reason: thou seest I am pacified
still. Nay prithee, be gone. *Exit Hostess.*

176 embossed: *swollen*   181 injuries; *cf. n.*

Now, Hal, to the news at court: for the robbery,
lad, how is that answered?   197

Prince. O! my sweet beef, I must still be good
angel to thee: the money is paid back again.

Fal. O! I do not like that paying back; 'tis
a double labour.   201

Prince. I am good friends with my father
and may do anything.

Fal. Rob me the exchequer the first thing
thou dost, and do it with unwashed hands too.

Bard. Do, my lord.

Prince. I have procured thee, Jack, a charge
of foot.   208

Fal. I would it had been of horse. Where
shall I find one that can steal well? O! for a
fine thief, of the age of two-and-twenty, or there-
abouts; I am heinously unprovided. Well, God
be thanked for these rebels; they offend none
but the virtuous: I laud them, I praise them.

Prince. Bardolph!

Bard. My lord?   216

Prince. Go bear this letter to Lord John of
    Lancaster,
To my brother John; this to my Lord of West-
    moreland.
Go, Peto, to horse, to horse! for thou and I
Have thirty miles to ride ere dinner-time.   220
Jack, meet me to-morrow in the Temple-hall
At two o'clock in the afternoon:
There shalt thou know thy charge, and there receive
Money and order for their furniture.   224
The land is burning; Percy stands on high;

205 unwashed hands; *cf. n.*   224 furniture: *equipment*

And either we or they must lower· lie.

   Fal. Rare words! brave world! Hostess, my breakfast; come!

O! I could wish this tavern were my drum.   228

                                    Exeunt omnes.

ACT FOURTH

Scene One

[Shrewsbury. The rebel camp]

Enter Harry Hotspur, Worcester, and Douglas.

   Hot. Well said, my noble Scot: if speaking truth
In this fine age were not thought flattery,
Such attribution should the Douglas have,
As not a soldier of this season's stamp   4
Should go so general current through the world.
By God, I cannot flatter; do defy
The tongues of soothers; but a braver place
In my heart's love hath no man than yourself.   8
Nay, task me to my word; approve me, lord.

   Doug. Thou art the the king of honour:
No man so potent breathes upon the ground
But I will beard him.

   Hot.   Do so, and 'tis well.   12

Enter a Messenger.

What letters hast thou there? I can but thank you.

   Mess. These letters come from your father.

   Hot. Letters from him! why comes he not himself?

---

228 drum; *cf. n.*   3 attribution: *praise*   4-5 *Cf. n.*
6 defy: *despise*   7 soothers: *flatterers*
9 task me to my word: *challenge me to make good my word*   approve:
  test

Mess. He cannot come, my lord: he's grievous
   sick.   16

Hot. 'Zounds! how'has he the leisure to be sick
In such a justling time? Who leads his power?
Under whose government come they along?

Mess. His letters bear his mind, not I, my lord. 20
Wor. I prithee, tell me, doth he keep his bed?
Mess. He did, my lord, four days ere I set forth;
And at the time of my departure thence
He was much fear'd by his physicians.   24

Wor. I would the state of time had first been whole
Ere he by sickness had been visited:
His health was never better worth than now.

Hot. Sick now! droop now! this sickness doth
   infect   28
The very life-blood of our enterprise;
'Tis catching hither, even to our camp.
He writes me here, that inward sickness——
And that his friends by deputation could not   32
So soon be drawn; nor did he think it meet
To lay so dangerous and dear a trust
On any soul remov'd but on his own.
Yet doth he give us bold advertisement,   36
That with our small conjunction we should on,
To see how fortune is dispos'd to us;
For, as he writes, there is no quailing now,
Because the king is certainly possess'd   40
Of all our purposes. What say you to it?

Wor. Your father's sickness is a maim to us.
Hot. A perilous gash, a very limb lopp'd off:
And yet, in faith, 'tis not; his present want   44
Seems more than we shall find it. Were it good

18 justling: *busy*   36 advertisement: *advice*
37 conjunction: *united forces*   40 possess'd: *informed*
44 his present want: *his absence now*

To set the exact wealth of all our states
All at one cast? to set so rich a main
On the nice hazard of one doubtful hour? 48
It were not good; for therein should we read
The very bottom and the soul of hope,
The very list, the very utmost bound
Of all our fortunes.

 Doug.   Faith, and so we should; 52
Where now remains a sweet reversion:
We may boldly spend upon the hope of what
Is to come in:
A comfort of retirement lives in this. 56

 Hot. A rendezvous, a home to fly unto,
If that the devil and mischance look big
Upon the maidenhead of our affairs.

 Wor. But yet, I would your father had been
  here. · 60
The quality and hair of our attempt
Brooks no division. It will be thought
By some, that know not why he is away,
That wisdom, loyalty, and mere dislike 64
Of our proceedings, kept the earl from hence.
And think how such an apprehension
May turn the tide of fearful faction
And breed a kind of question in our cause; 68
For well you know we of the offering side
Must keep aloof from strict arbitrement,
And stop all sight-holes, every loop from whence
The eye of reason may pry in upon us: 72
This absence of your father's draws a curtain,
That shows the ignorant a kind of fear

47 main: *stake*   48 nice: *slender, precarious*
51 list: *limit*   53, 56 *Cf. n.*   61 hair: *nature*
67 fearful: *timid*   69 the offering side: *the offensive*
70 arbitrement: *judicial inquiry*   73 draws: *draws aside*

Before not dreamt of.
   Hot.   You strain too far.
I rather of his absence make this use: 76
It lends a lustre and more great opinion,
A larger dare to our great enterprise,
Than if the earl were here; for men must think,
If we without his help can make a head   80
To push against the kingdom, with his help
We shall o'erturn it topsy-turvy down.
Yet all goes well, yet all our joints are whole.
   Doug. As heart can think: there is not such a
     word   84
Spoke of in Scotland as this term of fear.

       Enter Sir Richard Vernon.

   Hot. My cousin Vernon! welcome, by my soul.
   Ver. Pray God my news be worth a welcome, lord.
The Earl of Westmoreland, seven thousand strong,
Is marching hitherwards; with him Prince John.
   Hot. No harm: what more?
   Ver.   And further, I have learn'd,
The king himself in person is set forth,
Or hitherwards intended speedily,   92
With strong and mighty preparation.
   Hot. He shall be welcome too. Where is his son,
The nimble-footed madcap Prince of Wales,
And his comrades, that daff'd the world aside,   96
And bid it pass?
   Ver.   All furnish'd, all in arms,
All plum'd like estridges that with the wind
Baited like eagles having lately bath'd,
Glittering in golden coats, like images,   100
As full of spirit as the month of May,

77 opinion: *reputation*   96 daff'd: *thrust*
97 furnish'd: *equipped*   98-99 *Cf. n.*   100 *Cf. n.*

And gorgeous as the sun at midsummer,
Wanton as youthful goats, wild as young bulls.
I saw young Harry, with his beaver on,　　　　　104
His cushes on his thighs, gallantly arm'd,
Rise from the ground like feather'd Mercury,
And vaulted with such ease into his seat,
As if an angel dropp'd down from the clouds,
To turn and wind a fiery Pegasus　　　　　109
And witch the world with noble horsemanship.
　　Hot. No more, no more: worse than the sun in
　　　March
This praise doth nourish agues. Let them come;
They come like sacrifices in their trim,　　　　113
And to the fire-ey'd maid of smoky war
All hot and bleeding will we offer them:
The mailed Mars shall on his altar sit　　　　116
Up to the ears in blood. I am on fire
To hear this rich reprisal is so nigh
And yet not ours. Come, let me taste my horse,
Who is to bear me like a thunderbolt　　　　120
Against the bosom of the Prince of Wales:
Harry to Harry shall, hot horse to horse,
Meet and ne'er part till one drop down a corse.
O! that Glendower were come.
　　Ver.　　　　　　　　There is more news:　124
I learn'd in Worcester, as I rode along,
He cannot draw his power these fourteen days.
　　Doug. That's the worst tidings that I hear of yet.
　　Wor. Ay, by my faith, that bears a frosty
　　　sound.　　　　　　　　　　　　　128
　　Hot. What may the king's whole battle reach unto?
　　Ver. To thirty thousand.

104 beaver: *helmet*　　　　　105 cushes: *cuisses, thigh-armor*
109 wind: *wheel round*　　　　　　111-112 *Cf. n.*
113 trim: *trappings*　　　　　　118 reprisal: *prize*

Hot.   Forty let it be:
My father and Glendower being both away,
The powers of us may serve so great a day.   132
Come, let us take a muster speedily:
Doomsday is near; die all, die merrily.
  Doug. Talk not of dying: I am out of fear
Of death or death's hand for this one half year.

Exeunt Omnes.

Scene Two

[<i>A Road near Coventry</i>]

Enter Falstaff and Bardolph.

  Fal. Bardolph, get thee before to Coventry;
fill me a bottle of sack: our soldiers shall march
through: we'll to Sutton-Co'fil' to-night.
  Bard. Will you give me money, captain?   4
  Fal. Lay out, lay out.
  Bard. This bottle makes an angel.
  Fal. An if it do, take it for thy labour; and
if it make twenty, take them all, I'll answer the
coinage.   Bid my Lieutenant Peto meet me at
the town's end.   10
  Bard. I will, captain: farewell.   Exit.
  Fal. If I be not ashamed of my soldiers, I am
a soused gurnet.   I have misused the king's press
damnably.   I have got, in exchange of a hundred
and fifty soldiers, three hundred and odd pounds.
I press me none but good householders, yeomen's
sons; inquire me out contracted bachelors, such
as had been asked twice on the banns; such a

Sutton-Co'fil'; <i>cf. n.</i>   6 makes an angel; <i>cf. n.</i>
3 soused gurnet: <i>pickled fish</i>   king's press: <i>royal warrant for</i>
   conscripting troops
5 yeomen's: <i>small freeholders'</i>   17 contracted: i.e., <i>to be married</i>
3-19 <i>Cf. n.</i>

commodity of warm slaves, as had as lief hear the
devil as a drum; such as fear the report of a 20
caliver worse than a struck fowl or a hurt wild-
duck. I pressed me none but such toasts-and-
butter, with hearts in their bellies no bigger than
pins' heads, and they have bought out their services; and now my whole charge consists of
ancients, corporals, lieutenants, gentlemen of
companies, slaves as ragged as Lazarus in the
painted cloth, where the glutton's dogs licked his
sores; and such as indeed were never soldiers, but
discarded unjust serving-men, younger sons to 30
younger brothers, revolted tapsters and ostlers
trade-fallen, the cankers of a calm world and a
long peace; ten times more dishonourable ragged
than an old faced ancient: and such have I, to
fill up the rooms of them that have bought out
their services, that you would think that I had a
hundred and fifty tattered prodigals, lately come
from swine-keeping, from eating draff and husks.
A mad fellow met me on the way and told me I
had unloaded all the gibbets and pressed the 40
dead bodies. No eye hath seen such scarecrows.
I'll not march through Coventry with them,
that's flat: nay, and the villains march wide betwixt the legs, as if they had gyves on; for, indeed I had the most of them out of prison.
There's but a shirt and a half in all my company; and the half shirt is two napkins tacked
together and thrown over the shoulders like a

---

19 commodity: *stock*   warm: *luxury-loving*
21 caliver: *musket*   26 ancients: *ensigns*
27 Lazarus; *cf. III. iii. 36, n.*
28 painted cloth: *hangings decorated with figures*   32 cankers: *worms*
34 faced ancient: *patched flag*   37 prodigals; *cf. n.*
38 draff: *pig-wash*   44 gyves: *fetters*

herald's coat without sleeves; and the shirt, to
say the truth, stolen from my host at Saint
Alban's, or the red-nose inn-keeper of Daventry.
But that's all one; they'll find linen enough on
every hedge. 53

Enter the Prince, and the Lord of Westmoreland.

Prince. How now, blown Jack! how now,
quilt!

Fal. What, Hal! How now, mad wag! what a
devil dost thou in Warwickshire? My good Lord
of Westmoreland, I cry you mercy: I thought
your honour had already been at Shrewsbury.

West. Faith, Sir John, 'tis more than time
that I were there, and you too; but my powers
are there already. The king, I can tell you, looks
for us all: we must away all night. 63

Fal. Tut, never fear me: I am as vigilant as
a cat to steal cream.

Prince. I think to steal cream indeed, for
thy theft hath already made thee butter. But
tell me, Jack, whose fellows are these that come
after?

Fal. Mine, Hal, mine. 70

Prince. I did never see such pitiful rascals.

Fal. Tut, tut; good enough to toss; food for
powder, food for powder; they'll fill a pit as well
as better: tush, man, mortal men, mortal men.

West. Ay, but, Sir John, methinks they are
exceeding poor and bare; too beggarly. 76

Fal. Faith, for their poverty, I know not
where they had that; and for their bareness, I
am sure they never learned that of me. 79

54 blown: *swollen*
58 cry you mercy: *beg your pardon*   72 to toss: i.e., *upon a pike*

Prince. No, I'll be sworn; unless you call three fingers on the ribs bare. But sirrah, make haste: Percy is already in the field.

Fal. What, is the king encamped?

West. He is, Sir John: I fear we shall stay too
    long.   84

Fal. Well,

To the latter end of a fray and the beginning of a
    feast

Fits a dull fighter and a keen guest.   *Exeunt.*

Scene Three

[*Shrewsbury. The rebel camp*]

Enter Hotspur, Worcester, Douglas, and Vernon.

Hot. We'll fight with him to-night.

Wor.   It may not be.

Doug. You give him then advantage.

Ver.   Not a whit.

Hot. Why say you so? looks he not for supply?

Ver. So do we.

Hot.   His is certain, ours is doubtful.   4

Wor. Good cousin, be advis'd: stir not to-night.

Ver. Do not, my lord.

Doug.   You do not counsel well:

You speak it out of fear and cold heart.

Ver. Do me no slander, Douglas: by my life,—

And I dare well maintain it with my life,—   9

If well-respected honour bid me on,

I hold as little counsel with weak fear

As you, my lord, or any Scot that this day lives:

Let it be seen to-morrow in the battle_   13

Which of us fears.

---

84 stay: *linger*   10 well-respected: *well-considered, reasonable*

Doug.   Yea, or to-night.
Ver.   Content.
Hot. To-night, say I.
Ver. Come, come, it may not be. I wonder
　　much,   16
Being men of such great leading as you are,
That you foresee not what impediments
Drag back our expedition: certain horse
Of my cousin Vernon's are not yet come up: 20
Your uncle Worcester's horse came but to-day;
And now their pride and mettle is asleep,
Their courage with hard labour tame and dull,
That not a horse is half the half of himself.   24
　　Hot. So are the horses of the enemy
In general, journey-bated and brought low:
The better part of ours are full of rest.
　　Wor. The number of the king exceedeth ours:
For God's sake, cousin, stay till all come in.   29

　　　　　　The trumpet sounds a parley.
　　　　　　Enter Sir Walter Blunt.

　　Blunt. I come with gracious offers from the king,
If you vouchsafe me hearing and respect.
　　Hot. Welcome, Sir Walter Blunt; and would to
　　　God   32
You were of our determination!
Some of us love you well; and even those some
Envy your great deservings and good name,
Because you are not of our quality,   36
But stand against us like an enemy.
　　Blunt. And God defend but still I should stand so,
So long as out of limit and true rule
You stand against anointed majesty.   40

17 leading: *generalship*   26 journey-bated: *wearied with travel*
31 respect: *attention* 36 quality: *profession, party* 38 defend: *forbid*

But, to my charge. The king hath sent to know
The nature of your griefs, and whereupon
You conjure from the breast of civil peace
Such bold hostility, teaching his duteous land   44
Audacious cruelty. If that the king
Have any way your good deserts forgot,—
Which he confesseth to be manifold,—
He bids you name your griefs; and with all speed   48
You shall have your desires with interest,
And pardon absolute for yourself and these
Herein misled by your suggestion.
 Hot. The king is kind; and well we know the
  king   52
Knows at what time to promise, when to pay.
My father and my uncle and myself
Did give him that same royalty he wears;
And when he was not six-and-twenty strong,   56
Sick in the world's regard, wretched and low,
A poor unminded outlaw sneaking home,
My father gave him welcome to the shore;
And when he heard him swear and vow to God
He came but to be Duke of Lancaster,   61
To sue his livery and beg his peace,
With tears of innocency and terms of zeal,
My father, in kind heart and pity mov'd,   64
Swore him assistance and perform'd it too.
Now when the lords and barons of the realm
Perceiv'd Northumberland did lean to him,
The more and less came in with cap and knee;
Met him in boroughs, cities, villages,   69
Attended him on bridges, stood in lanes,
Laid gifts before him, proffer'd him their oaths,

51 suggestion: *instigation*
62 sue his livery: *bring suit for the delivery of his lands*
68 more and less: *great and small*   70 attended: *awaited*

Gave him their heirs as pages, follow'd him   72
Even at the heels in golden multitudes.
He presently, as greatness knows itself,
Steps me a little higher than his vow
Made to my father, while his blood was poor,   76
Upon the naked shore at Ravenspurgh;
And now, forsooth, takes on him to reform
Some certain edicts and some strait decrees
That lie too heavy on the commonwealth,   80
Cries out upon abuses, seems to weep
Over his country's wrongs; and by this face,
This seeming brow of justice, did he win
The hearts of all that he did angle for;   84
Proceeded further; cut me off the heads
Of all the favourites that the absent king
In deputation left behind him here,
When he was personal in the Irish war.   88
    Blunt. Tut, I came not to hear this.
    Hot.   Then to the point.
In short time after, he depos'd the king;
Soon after that, depriv'd him of his life;
And, in the neck of that, task'd the whole state;
To make that worse, suffer'd his kinsman March—   93
Who is, if every owner were well plac'd,
Indeed his king—to be engag'd in Wales,
There without ransom to lie forfeited;   96
Disgrac'd me in my happy victories;
Sought to entrap me by intelligence;
Rated my uncle from the council-board;
In rage dismiss'd my father from the court;   100
Broke oath on oath, committed wrong on wrong;

79 strait: *strict*   88 personal: *in person*   92 task'd: *taxed*
95 engag'd: *held as hostage*
98 intelligence: *information obtained through spies*
99 rated: *drove away by chiding*

And in conclusion drove us to seek out
This head of safety; and withal to pry
Into his title, the which we find   104
Too indirect for long continuance.
    Blunt. Shall I return this answer to the king?
    Hot. Not so, Sir Walter: we'll withdraw awhile.
Go to the king; and let there be impawn'd   108
Some surety for a safe return again,
And in the morning early shall my uncle
Bring him our purposes; and so farewell.
    Blunt. I would you would accept of grace and
      love.   112
    Hot. And may be so we shall.
    Blunt.   Pray God, you do!
                                    Exeunt.

Scene Four

[*York.   The Archbishop's Palace*]

Enter the Archbishop of York and Sir Michael.

    Arch. Hie, good Sir Michael; bear this sealed brief
With winged haste to the lord marshal;
This to my cousin Scroop, and all the rest
To whom they are directed. If you knew   4
How much they do import, you would make haste.
    Sir M. My good lord,
I guess their tenour.
    Arch.   Like enough you do.
To-morrow, good Sir Michael, is a day   8
Wherein the fortune of ten thousand men
Must bide the touch; for, sir, at Shrewsbury,
As I am truly given to understand,
The king with mighty and quick-raised power   12

103 head of safety: *army for protection*   105 indirect: *crooked*
1 brief: *letter*   10 bide the touch: *be put to the test*

Meets with Lord Harry: and, I fear, Sir Michael,
What with the sickness of Northumberland,—
Whose power was in the first proportion,—
And what with Owen Glendower's absence thence,   16
Who with them was a rated sinew too,
And comes not in, o'er-rul'd by prophecies,—
I fear the power of Percy is too weak
To wage an instant trial with the king.   20

    Sir M. Why, my good lord, you need not fear:
There is the Douglas and Lord Mortimer.

    Arch. No, Mortimer is not there.

    Sir M. But there is Mordake, Vernon, Lord Harry
      Percy,   24
And there's my Lord of Worcester, and a head
Of gallant warriors, noble gentlemen.

    Arch. And so there is; but yet the king hath drawn
The special head of all the land together: 28
The Prince of Wales, Lord John of Lancaster,
The noble Westmoreland, and war-like Blunt;
And many moe corrivals and dear men
Of estimation and command in arms.   32

    Sir M. Doubt not, my lord, they shall be well
      oppos'd.

    Arch. I hope no less, yet needful 'tis to fear;
And, to prevent the worse, Sir Michael, speed:
For if Lord Percy thrive not, ere the king   36
Dismiss his power, he means to visit us,
For he hath heard of our confederacy,
And 'tis but wisdom to make strong against him:
Therefore make haste. I must go write again   40
To other friends; and so farewell, Sir Michael.

                                Exeunt.

17 rated sinew: *strength on which they counted*
31 moe corrivals: *more comrades*   dear: *valued*
32 estimation: *reputation*

ACT FIFTH

Scene One

[Shrewsbury. The King's Camp]

Enter the King, Prince of Wales, Lord John of
  Lancaster, Sir Walter Blunt, and Falstaff.

King. How bloodily the sun begins to peer
Above yon busky hill! the day looks pale
At his distemperature.
Prince.   The southern wind
Doth play the trumpet to his purposes,   4
And by his hollow whistling in the leaves
Foretells a tempest and a blustering day.
  King. Then with the losers let it sympathize,
For nothing can seem foul to those that win.   8
                          The trumpet sounds.

Enter Worcester [and Vernon].

How now, my Lord of Worcester! 'tis not well
That you and I should meet upon such terms
As now we meet. You have deceiv'd our trust,
And made us doff our easy robes of peace,   12
To crush our old limbs in ungentle steel.
This is not well, my lord; this is not well.
What say you to it? will you again unknit
This churlish knot of all-abhorred war,.   16
And move in that obedient orb again
Where you did give a fair and natural light,
And be no more an exhal'd meteor,
A prodigy of fear and a portent   20

2 busky: *bushy*   3 distemperature: *inclemency, ill-humour*
13 old limbs; *cf. n.*   17 obedient orb: *sphere of obedience*
19 exhal'd: *drawn forth; especially vapours drawn forth by the sun*
  and producing meteors

Of broached mischief to the unborn times?
   Wor. Hear me, my liege.
For mine own part, I could be well content
To entertain the lag-end of my life   24
With quiet hours; for I do protest
I have not sought the day of this dislike.
   King. You have not sought it! how comes it then?
   Fal. Rebellion lay in his way, and he found it.
   Prince. Peace, chewet, peace!   29
   Wor. It pleas'd your majesty to turn your looks
Of favour from myself and all our house;
And yet I must remember you, my lord,   32
We were the first and dearest of your friends.
For you my staff of office did I break
In Richard's time; and posted day and night
To meet you on the way, and kiss your hand,   36
When yet you were in place and in account
Nothing so strong and fortunate as I.
It was myself, my brother, and his son,
That brought you home and boldly did outdare
The dangers of the time. You swore to us,   41
And you did swear that oath at Doncaster,
That you did nothing purpose 'gainst the state,
Nor claim no further than your new-fall'n right,
The seat of Gaunt, dukedom of Lancaster.   45
To this we swore our aid: but, in short space
It rain'd down fortune showering on your head,
And such a flood of greatness fell on you,   48
What with our help, what with the absent king,
What with the injuries of a wanton time,
The seeming sufferances that you had borne,
And the contrarious winds that held the king   52

21 broached: *begun*   29 chewet: *jackdaw* (?)
50 wanton time: *frivolous reign*   51 sufferances: *sufferings*

So long in his unlucky Irish wars,
That all in England did repute him dead:
And from this swarm of fair advantages
You took occasion to be quickly woo'd   56
To gripe the general sway into your hand;
Forgot your oath to us at Doncaster;
And being fed by us you us'd us so
As that ungentle gull, the cuckoo's bird,   60
Useth the sparrow: did oppress our nest,
Grew by our feeding to so great a bulk
That even our love durst not come near your sight
For fear of swallowing; but with nimble wing   64
We were enforc'd, for safety's sake, to fly
Out of your sight and raise this present head;
Whereby we stand opposed by such means
As you yourself have forg'd against yourself   68
By unkind usage, dangerous countenance,
And violation of all faith and troth
Sworn to us in your younger enterprise.
    King. These things indeed, you have articulate,   72
Proclaim'd at market-crosses, read in churches,
To face the garment of rebellion
With some fine colour that may please the eye
Of fickle changelings and poor discontents,   76
Which gape and rub the elbow at the news
Of hurlyburly innovation:
And never yet did insurrection want
Such water-colours to impaint his cause;   80
Nor moody beggars, starving for a time
Of pell-mell havoc and confusion.
    Prince. In both our armies there is many a soul
Shall pay full dearly for this encounter,   84

---

60 gull: *an unfledged nestling; cf. n.*   69 dangerous: *threatening*
72 articulate: *set forth in articles*
74 face: *trim*   78 innovation: *revolution*

If once they join in trial. Tell your nephew,
The Prince of Wales doth join with all the world
In praise of Henry Percy: by my hopes,
This present enterprise set off his head,   88
I do not think a braver gentleman,
More active-valiant or more valiant-young,
More daring or more bold, is now alive
To grace this latter age with noble deeds.   92
For my part, I may speak it to my shame,
I have a truant been to chivalry;
And so I hear he doth account me too;
Yet this before my father's majesty:—   96
I am content that he shall take the odds
Of his great name and estimation,
And will, to save the blood on either side,
Try fortune with him in a single fight.   100

   King. And, Prince of Wales, so dare we venture
    thee,
Albeit considerations infinite
Do make against it. No, good Worcester, no,
We love our people well; even those we love   104
That are misled upon your cousin's part;
And, will they take the offer of our grace,
Both he and they and you, yea, every man
Shall be my friend again, and I'll be his.   108
So tell your cousin, and bring me word
What he will do; but if he will not yield,
Rebuke and dread correction wait on us,
And they shall do their office. So, be gone: 112
We will not now be troubled with reply;
We offer fair, take it advisedly.

              Exit Worcester [*with Vernon*].

88 set off his head: *taken from his account*
111 wait on us: *are in our service*

Prince. It will not be accepted, on my life.
The Douglas and the Hotspur both together 116
Are confident against the world in arms.

King. Hence, therefore, every leader to his charge;
For, on their answer, will we set on them;
And God befriend us, as our cause is just! 120

Exeunt. Manet Prince and Falstaff.

Fal. Hal, if thou see me down in the battle,
and bestride me, so; 'tis a point of friendship.

Prince. Nothing but a colossus can do thee
that friendship. Say thy prayers, and farewell.

Fal. I would it were bed-time, Hal, and all
well. 126

Prince. Why, thou owest God a death.

[*Exit Prince.*]

Fal. 'Tis not due yet: I would be loath to
pay him before his day. What need I be so
forward with him that calls not on me? Well,
'tis no matter; honour pricks me on. Yea, but
how if honour prick me off when I come on?
how then? Can honour set to a leg? No. Or an
arm? No. Or take away the grief of a wound?
No. Honour hath no skill in surgery then? No.
What is honour? a word. What is that word,
honour? Air. A trim reckoning! Who hath it?
he that died o' Wednesday. Doth he feel it?
No. Doth he hear it? No. It is insensible
then? Yea, to the dead. But will it not live
with the living? No. Why? Detraction will not
suffer it. Therefore I'll none of it: honour is a
mere scutcheon; and so ends my catechism. 143

Exit.

127-128 *Cf. n.*
143 scutcheon: *shield with armorial bearings, carried in funeral pro-
cessions*

Scene Two

[Shrewsbury.   The Rebel Camp]

Enter Worcester and Sir Richard Vernon.

Wor. O, no! my nephew must not know, Sir
    Richard,
The liberal kind offer of the king.
    Ver. 'Twere best he did.
    Wor.   Then are we all undone.
It is not possible, it cannot be,   4
The king should keep his word in loving us;
He will suspect us still, and find a time
To punish this offence in other faults:
Suspicion all our lives shall be stuck full of eyes;   8
For treason is but trusted like the fox,
Who, ne'er so tame, so cherish'd, and lock'd up,
Will have a wild trick of his ancestors.
Look how we can, or sad or merrily,   12
Interpretation will misquote our looks,
And we shall feed like oxen at a stall,
The better cherish'd, still the nearer death.
My nephew's trespass may be well forgot,   16
It hath the excuse of youth and heat of blood;
And an adopted name of privilege,
A hare-brain'd Hotspur, govern'd by a spleen.
All his offences live upon my head   20
And on his father's: we did train him on;
And, his corruption being ta'en from us,
We, as the spring of all, shall pay for all.
Therefore, good cousin, let not Harry know   24
In any case the offer of the king.

18 adopted name of privilege: *nickname which carries certain privi-
leges with it*

Ver. Deliver what you will, I'll say 'tis so.
Here comes your cousin.

Enter Hotspur [and Douglas].

Hot. My uncle is return'd: deliver up   28
My Lord of Westmoreland.   Uncle, what news?
Wor. The king will bid you battle presently.
Doug. Defy him by the Lord of Westmoreland.
Hot. Lord Douglas, go you and tell him so.   32
Doug. Marry, and shall, and very willingly.

Exit Douglas.

Wor. There is no seeming mercy in the king.
Hot. Did you beg any?   God forbid!
Wor. I told him gently of our grievances,   36
Of his oath-breaking; which he mended thus,
By now forswearing that he is forsworn:
He calls us rebels, traitors; and will scourge
With haughty arms this hateful name in us.   40

Enter Douglas.

Doug. Arm, gentlemen! to arms! for I have thrown
A brave defiance in King Henry's teeth,
And Westmoreland, that was engag'd, did bear it;
Which cannot choose but bring him quickly on.
Wor. The Prince of Wales stepp'd forth before the
   king,   45
And, nephew, challeng'd you to single fight.
Hot. O! would the quarrel lay upon our heads,
And that no man might draw short breath to-day   48
But I and Harry Monmouth. Tell me, tell me,
How show'd his tasking? seem'd it in contempt?
Ver. No, by my soul; I never in my life
Did hear a challenge urg'd more modestly,   52

50 tasking: *challenge*

Unless a brother should a brother dare
To gentle exercise and proof of arms.
He gave you all the duties of a man,
Trimm'd up your praises with a princely tongue,
Spoke your deservings like a chronicle,   57
Making you ever better than his praise,
By still dispraising praise valu'd with you;
And, which became him like a prince indeed,   ·   60
He made a blushing cital of himself,
And chid his truant youth with such a grace
As if he master'd there a double spirit
Of teaching and of learning instantly.   64
There did he pause. But let me tell the world,
If he outlive the envy of this day,
England did never owe so sweet a hope,   .
So much misconstru'd in his wantonness.   68

   Hot. Cousin, I think thou art enamoured
On his follies: never did I hear
Of any prince so wild a libertine.
But be he as he will, yet once ere night   72
I will embrace him with a soldier's arm,
That he shall shrink under my courtesy.
Arm, arm, with speed! And, fellows, soldiers,
    friends,
Better consider what you have to do,   76
Than I, that have not well the gift of tongue, .
Can lift your blood up with persuasion.

        .   *Enter a Messenger.*

   Mess. My lord, here are letters for you.
    Hot. I cannot read them now.   80
O gentlemen! the time of life is short;
To spend that shortness basely were too long,

55 duties: *compliments*   61 cital of: *reference to*   67 owe: *own*

If life did ride upon a dial's point,
Still ending at the arrival of an hour.   84
An if we live, we live to tread on kings;
If die, brave death, when princes die with us!
Now, for our consciences, the arms are fair,
When the intent of bearing them is just.   88

Enter another Messenger.

Mess. My lord, prepare; the king comes on apace.
Hot. I thank him that he cuts me from my tale,
For I profess not talking. Only this,—
Let each man do his best: and here draw I   92
A sword, whose temper I intend to stain
With the best blood that I can meet withal
In the adventure of this perilous day.
Now, *Esperance!* Percy! and set on.   96
Sound all the lofty instruments of war,
And by that music let us all embrace;
For, heaven to earth, some of us never shall
A second time do such a courtesy.   100

Here they embrace; the trumpets sound.
[*Exeunt.*]

[Scene Three

The battle field]

*The King entereth with his power. Alarum unto the
    battle. Then enter Douglas and Sir Walter
    Blunt.*

Blunt. What is thy name, that in the battle thus
Thou crossest me? what honour dost thou seek
Upon my head?
Doug.   Know then, my name is Douglas;

83 dial's point: *hand of a clock*

And I do haunt thee in the battle thus   4
Because some tell me that thou art a king.
   Blunt. They tell thee true.
   Doug. The Lord of Stafford dear to-day hath
     bought
Thy likeness; for, instead of thee, King Harry,   8
This sword hath ended him: so shall it thee,
Unless thou yield thee as my prisoner.
   Blunt. I was not born a yielder, thou proud Scot;
And thou shalt find a king that will revenge   12
Lord Stafford's death.
                They fight. Douglas kills Blunt.
                 Then enter Hotspur.
   Hot. O, Douglas, hadst thou fought at Holmedon
     thus,
I never had triumph'd upon a Scot.
   Doug. All's done, all's won: here breathless lies
     the king.   16
   Hot. Where?
   Doug. Here.
   Hot. This, Douglas! no; I know this face full
     well;
A gallant knight he was, his name was Blunt;   20
Semblably furnish'd like the king himself.
   Doug. A fool go with thy soul, whither it goes!
A borrow'd title hast thou bought too dear:
Why didst thou tell me that thou wert a king?
   Hot. The king hath many marching in his coats. 25
   Doug. Now, by my sword, I will kill all his coats;
I'll murder all his wardrobe, piece by piece,
Until I meet the king.
   Hot.   Up, and away!   28
Our soldiers stand full fairly for the day.   *Exeunt.*

21 Semblably furnish'd: *dressed to resemble*

Alarum, and enter Falstaff, solus.

Fal. Though I could 'scape shot-free at
London, I fear the shot here; here's no scoring
but upon the pate. Soft! who art thou? Sir
Walter Blunt: there's honour for you! here's
no vanity! I am as hot as molten lead, and as
heavy too: God keep lead out of me! I need
no more weight than mine own bowels. I have
led my ragamuffins where they are peppered:
there's not three of my hundred and fifty left
alive, and they are for the town's end, to beg
during life. But who comes here?   40

Enter the Prince.

Prince. What! stand'st thou idle here? lend me thy
      sword:
Many a nobleman lies stark and stiff
Under the hoofs of vaunting enemies,
Whose deaths are unreveng'd: prithee, lend me thy
      sword.   44

Fal. O Hal! I prithee, give me leave to
breathe awhile. Turk Gregory never did such
deeds in arms as I have done this day. I have
paid Percy, I have made him sure.   48

Prince. He is indeed; and living to kill thee.
I prithee, lend me thy sword.

Fal. Nay, before God, Hal, if Percy be alive,
thou gett'st not my sword; but take my pistol,
if thou wilt.   53

Prince. Give it me. What! is it in the case?

Fal. Ay, Hal; 'tis hot, 'tis hot: there's that
will sack a city.

---

30 shot-free: *without having to pay*   46 Turk Gregory; *cf. n.*

> *The Prince draws it out, and*
> *finds it to be a bottle of sack.*

Prince. What! is 't a time to jest and dally now?

> *He throws the bottle at him.   Exit.*

Fal. Well, if Percy be alive, I'll pierce him. If he do come in my way, so: if he do not, if I come in his, willingly, let him make a carbonado of me.   I like not such grinning honour as Sir Walter hath: give me life; which if I can save, so; if not, honour comes unlooked for, and there's an end.   *Exit.*

Scene [Four

The battle field]

Alarums.   Excursions.   Enter the King, the Prince, Lord John of Lancaster, and Earl of Westmoreland.

King. I prithee,
Harry, withdraw thyself; thou bleed'st too much.
Lord John of Lancaster, go you with him.

Lanc. Not I, my lord, unless I did bleed too.   4

Prince. I beseech your majesty, make up,
Lest your retirement do amaze your friends.

King. I will do so.
My Lord of Westmoreland, lead him to his tent.   8

West. Come, my lord, I'll lead you to your tent.

Prince. Lead me, my lord?   I do not need your help:
And God forbid a shallow scratch should drive
The Prince of Wales from such a field as this,   12

---

58 pierce; *cf. n.*   60 carbonado: *a piece of meat slashed for broiling*
5 make up: *go forward*   6 amaze: *confound, alarm*

Where stain'd nobility lies trodden on,
And rebels' arms triumph in massacres!
   Lanc. We breathe too long: come, cousin West-
    moreland,
Our duty this way lies: for God's sake, come.   16
                [Exeunt Lord John of Lancaster
                    and Earl of Westmoreland.]
   Prince. By God, thou hast deceiv'd me, Lancaster;
I did not think thee lord of such a spirit:
Before, I lov'd thee as a brother, John;
But now, I do respect thee as my soul.   20
   King. I saw him hold Lord Percy at the point
With lustier maintenance than I did look for
Of such an ungrown warrior.
   Prince.   O! this boy
Lends mettle to us all.   *Exit.*

          Enter Douglas.

   Doug. Another king! they grow like Hydra's
    heads: 25
I am the Douglas, fatal to all those
That wear those colours on them: what art thou,
That counterfeit'st the person of a king?   28
   King. The king himself; who, Douglas, grieves at
    heart
So many of his shadows thou hast met
And not the very king. I have two boys
Seek Percy and thyself about the field: 32
But, seeing thou fall'st on me so luckily,
I will assay thee; so defend thyself.
   Doug. I fear thou art another counterfeit;
And yet, in faith, thou bear'st thee like a king:

22 lustier maintenance: *more vigorous bearing*
25 Hydra: *a fabled monster, whose heads grew again as they were
    cut off*

But mine I am sure thou art, whoe'er thou be,
And thus I win thee.

> *They fight. The King being*
> *in danger, enter Prince.*

Prince. Hold up thy head, vile Scot, or thou art
  like
Never to hold it up again! the spirits   40
Of valiant Shirley, Stafford, Blunt, are in my arms:
It is the Prince of Wales that threatens thee,
Who never promiseth but he means to pay.

> *They fight: Douglas flieth.*

Cheerly, my lord: how fares your Grace?   44
Sir Nicholas Gawsey hath for succour sent,
And so hath Clifton: I'll to Clifton straight.

King. Stay, and breathe awhile.
Thou hast redeem'd thy lost opinion,   48
And show'd thou mak'st some tender of my life,
In this fair rescue thou hast brought to me.

Prince. O God! they did me too much injury
That ever said I hearken'd for your death.   52
If it were so, I might have let alone
The insulting hand of Douglas over you;
Which would have been as speedy in your end
As all the poisonous potions in the world,   56
And sav'd the treacherous labour of your son.

King. Make up to Clifton: I'll to Sir Nicholas
  Gawsey.   *Exit.*

Enter Hotspur.

Hot. If I mistake not, thou art Harry Monmouth.
Prince. Thou speak'st as if I would deny my
  name.   60
Hot. My name is Harry Percy.

49 mak'st some tender: *hast some regard for*
52 hearken'd for: *watched for, desired*

Prince. Why, then, I see
A very valiant rebel of that name.
I am the Prince of Wales; and think not, Percy,
To share with me in glory any more: 64
Two stars keep not their motion in one sphere;
Nor can one England brook a double reign,
Of Harry Percy and the Prince of Wales.

Hot. Nor shall it, Harry; for the hour is come 68
To end the one of us; and would to God
Thy name in arms were now as great as mine!

Prince. I'll make it greater ere I part from thee;
And all the budding honours on thy crest 72
I'll crop, to make a garland for my head.

Hot. I can no longer brook thy vanities.

> *They fight. Enter Falstaff.*

Fal. Well said, Hal! to it, Hal! Nay, you
shall find no boy's play here, I can tell you. 76

> *Enter Douglas. He fights with Falstaff, who
> falls down as if he were dead. [Exit
> Douglas]. The Prince killeth Percy.*

Hot. O, Harry! thou hast robb'd me of my youth.
I better brook the loss of brittle life
Than those proud titles thou hast won of me;
They wound my thoughts worse than thy sword my
    flesh: 80
But thought's the slave of life, and life time's fool;
And time, that takes survey of all the world,
Must have a stop. O! I could prophesy,
But that the earthy and cold hand of death 84
Lies on my tongue. No, Percy, thou art dust,
And food for— [*Dies.*]

Prince. For worms, brave Percy. Fare thee well,
    great heart!

65 *Cf. n.* 81-83 *Cf. n.*

Ill-weav'd ambition, how much art thou shrunk!
When that this body did contain a spirit,   89
A kingdom for it was too small a bound;
But now, two paces of the vilest earth
Is room enough: this earth, that bears thee dead,   92
Bears not alive so stout a gentleman.
If thou wert sensible of courtesy,
I should not make so dear a show of zeal:
But let my favours hide thy mangled face,   96
And, even in thy behalf, I'll thank myself
For doing these fair rites of tenderness.
Adieu, and take thy praise with thee to heaven!
Thy ignominy sleep with thee in the grave,   100
But not remember'd in thy epitaph!
                    He spieth Falstaff on the ground.
What! old acquaintance! could not all this flesh
Keep in a little life?   Poor Jack, farewell!
I could have better spar'd a better man.   104
O! I should have a heavy miss of thee
If I were much in love with vanity.
Death hath not struck so fat a deer to-day,
Though many dearer, in this bloody fray.   108
Embowell'd will I see thee by and by:
Till then in blood by noble Percy lie.   *Exit.*

                Falstaff riseth up.

    Fal. Embowelled! if thou embowel me to-
day, I'll give you leave to powder me and
eat me too, to-morrow.   'Sblood! 'twas time to
counterfeit, or that hot termagant Scot had paid
me scot and lot too.   Counterfeit?   I lie, I am no

93 stout: *valiant*   95 dear: *affectionate*
96 favours: *a knot of ribbons worn by a knight, the gift of his lady*
109 Embowell'd: *disembowelled for embalming*
112 powder: *salt*   114 termagant: *violent; cf. n.*
115 scot and lot: *a tax paid according to one's ability and resources*

counterfeit: to die, is to be a counterfeit; for he
is but the counterfeit of a man, who hath not
the life of a man; but to counterfeit dying, when
a man thereby liveth, is to be no counterfeit, but
the true and perfect image of life indeed. The
better part of valour is discretion; in the which
better part, I have saved my life. 'Zounds! I
am afraid of this gunpowder Percy though he
be dead: how, if he should counterfeit too and
rise? By my faith I am afraid he would prove
the better counterfeit. Therefore I'll make him
sure; yea, and I'll swear I killed him. Why may
not he rise as well as I? Nothing confutes me
but eyes, and nobody sees me: therefore, sirrah,
with a new wound in your thigh come you along
with me.

He takes up Hotspur on his back.
Enter Prince and John of Lancaster.

Prince. Come, brother John; full bravely hast thou
  flesh'd   132
Thy maiden sword.

Lanc.   But, soft! whom have we here?
Did you not tell me this fat man was dead?

Prince. I did; I saw him dead,
Breathless and bleeding on the ground.   136
Art thou alive? or is it fantasy
That plays upon our eyesight? I prithee, speak;
We will not trust our eyes without our ears:
Thou art not what thou seem'st.   140

Fal. No, that's certain; I am not a double
man: but if I be not Jack Falstaff, then am I a
Jack. There is Percy: if your father will do
me any honour, so; if not, let him kill the

next Percy himself. I look to be either earl or
duke, I can assure you.

Prince. Why, Percy I killed myself, and saw thee
   dead.   147

   Fal. Didst thou? Lord, Lord! how this world
is given to lying. I grant you I was down and
out of breath, and so was he; but we rose both
at an instant, and fought a long hour by Shrewsbury clock. If I may be believed, so; if not, let
them that should reward valour bear the sin
upon their own heads. I'll take it upon my
death, I gave him this wound in the thigh: if
the man were alive and would deny it, 'zounds,
I would make him eat a piece of my sword.   157

Lanc. This is the strangest tale that e'er I heard.

Prince. This is the strangest fellow, brother John.
Come, bring your luggage nobly on your back:
For my part, if a lie may do thee grace,   161
I'll gild it with the happiest terms I have.

                   A retreat is sounded.
The trumpet sounds retreat; the day is ours.
Come, brother, let us to the highest of the field,
To see what friends are living, who are dead.   165

                             Exeunt.

   Fal. I'll follow, as they say, for reward. He
that rewards me, God reward him! If I do grow
great, I'll grow less; for I'll purge, and leave
sack, and live cleanly, as a nobleman should do.

                               Exit.

Scene [Five

The battle field]

Enter the King, Prince of Wales, Lord John of Lancaster, Earl of Westmoreland, with Worcester and Vernon, prisoners.

King. Thus ever did rebellion find rebuke.
Ill-spirited Worcester! did we not send grace,
Pardon, and terms of love to all of you?
And wouldst thou turn our offers contrary?   4
Misuse the tenour of thy kinsman's trust?
Three knights upon our party slain to-day,
A noble earl and many a creature else
Had been alive this hour,   8
If like a Christian, thou hadst truly borne
Betwixt our armies true intelligence.

Wor. What I have done my safety urg'd me to;
And I embrace this fortune patiently,   12
Since not to be avoided it falls on me.

King. Bear Worcester to the death and Vernon
    too:
Other offenders we will pause upon.

             Exit Worcester and Vernon.

How goes the field?   16

Prince. The noble Scot, Lord Douglas, when he
    saw
The fortune of the day quite turn'd from him,
The noble Percy slain, and all his men
Upon the foot of fear, fled with the rest;   20
And falling from a hill he was so bruis'd
That the pursuers took him. At my tent

20 Upon the foot of fear: *flying in fear*

The Douglas is, and I beseech your Grace
I may dispose of him.
　　King.　　　　　　　With all my heart.　　24
　　Prince. Then, brother. John of Lancaster, to you
This honourable bounty shall belong.
Go to the Douglas, and deliver him
Up to his pleasure, ransomless, and free:　　　28
His valour shown upon our crests to-day
Hath taught us how to cherish such high deeds,
Even in the bosom of our adversaries.
　　Lanc. I ` thank your Grace for this high cour-
　　　　tesy,　　　　　　　　　　　　　　　32
Which I shall give away immediately.
　　King. Then this remains, that we divide our power.
You, son John, and my cousin Westmoreland
Towards York shall bend you, with your dearest
　　　　speed,　　　　　　　　　　　　　36
To meet Northumberland and the prelate Scroop,
Who, as we hear, are busily in arms:⁻
Myself and you, son Harry, will towards Wales,
To fight with Glendower and the Earl of March.
Rebellion in this land shall lose his sway,　　41
Meeting the check of such another day:
And since this business so fair is done,
Let us not leave till all our own be won.　　*Exeunt.*

36 dearest: *best*

NOTES

I. i. 5. *entrance of this soil.* The earth is personified, and the dry surface is called her mouth.

I. i. 28. Cf. the last lines of Shakespeare's *Richard II*, King Henry's speech when news is brought him that, at his suggestion, King Richard, his predecessor whose throne he has usurped, has been murdered:

> Lords, I protest, my soul is full of woe
> That blood should sprinkle me to make me grow:
> Come, mourn with me for that I do lament
> And put on sullen black incontinent:
> I'll make a journey to the Holy Land
> To wash this blood from off my guilty hand.

During the year which has intervened, civil wars have prevented the fulfilment of this vow.

I. i. 38. *Mortimer,* Earl of March, rightful heir to the throne of England at the time of King Richard's death (see genealogical table in note on I. iii. 145-146), now in command of King Henry's forces on the western front.

I. i. 52. *Holy-rood day.* Holy Cross Day, September 14.

I. i. 53. *Young Harry Percy.* The youngest member of the great Percy family, now in command of the king's forces on the northern front. The Percies (see Dramatis Personæ) had been King Henry's chief supporters in his usurpation of the throne.

I. i. 71. *Mordake, the Earl of Fife,* was not son to beaten Douglas, but to the Duke of Albany, regent of Scotland. Shakespeare's error is due to a mistake in punctuation in Holinshed's list of Hotspur's prisoners, which reads: 'Mordacke earle of Fife, son to the governour Archembald earle Dowglas, etc.' A comma was omitted after 'governour,' and Shakespeare understood that 'Archembald' was 'governour.'

I. i. 91-95. By the law of arms, the King might claim only such prisoners as were of royal blood, and the historical Hotspur was therefore entirely within his rights in refusing to send to the king any prisoners except Mordake. But Shakespeare did not know that Mordake was of royal blood (see preceding note) and he was apparently ignorant of the law of arms which gave Hotspur the right to keep the rest of the prisoners. No attempt is made to explain why Shakespeare's Hotspur sent Mordake to the king—Shakespeare merely follows the facts as set down in Holinshed. The indignation of King Henry and Westmoreland, in this scene, at 'young Percy's pride'; Hotspur's conciliatory tone and his explanations when he appears at court (I. iii.); and the fact that neither Hotspur nor his uncle, Worcester, the experienced diplomat, ever suggests that Hotspur has a legal right to his prisoners; all these things indicate that Shakespeare's Hotspur is not within his rights in keeping the prisoners. His refusal was, at first, a thoughtless and impetuous act; and the refusal once made, the shrewd Worcester saw reasons for influencing his nephew to stand by this first hasty reply to the king's demand.

I. i. 97. *Malevolent to you in all aspects.* An astrological allusion, referring to the supposed good and evil influences of the planets. The king uses an astrological figure in his address to Worcester in V. i. 17-21.

I. i. 107. *uttered* is used here in its peculiar Elizabethan sense, namely, to put into circulation or to offer to the public. The substance of the king's speech is: 'Dismiss the lords until Wednesday next, but you yourself return to me at once, for more is to be said and done, than I can say or do *in public* in my present angry condition.'

I. ii. 16. *seven stars.* The Pleiades; also a common tavern-sign.

I. ii. 16. *wandering knight.* El Donzel del Febo, Knight of the Sun (or Phœbus), hero of a popular Spanish romance. This quotation is perhaps from some contemporary ballad founded on the romance.

I. ii. 19-33. Falstaff plays on the word Grace, using it first as a title, then in reference to the spiritual state of grace, and finally as 'grace before meat.' From this simple pun he proceeds to a more complicated play on words. There is the obvious play on *night* and *knight* in l. 27, followed in l. 28 by the play on the words *body, beauty,* and *booty,* in each of which the vowel sound, in Shakespeare's day, approximated the round *o* sound, as in *note.* Finally there is the play on the phrase *under whose countenance.*

I. ii. 49. Hal's quibble on the word durance would have greater significance if a buff jerkin were the costume of a prisoner instead of the ordinary dress of a sheriff's officer. The ideas of a sheriff and 'durance vile' are closely enough associated, however, to give some point to the jest.

I. ii. 87. Eating the flesh of a hare was supposed to generate melancholy.

I. ii. 88. *Moor-ditch* was a stagnant ditch and morass outside the walls of London.

I. ii. 101. *damnable iteration.* A damnable trick of quoting and misapplying.

I. ii. 118. *Gadshill.* The name of one of the robbers and of the place of the robbery.

I. ii. 144. *Eastcheap.* The district in London where the Boar's Head Tavern, the rendezvous of Hal and Falstaff, was situated.

I. ii. 177. *All-hallown summer.* The warm weather which comes at about the time of All Saints' Day, November first; called in America Indian Summer. The reference is to Falstaff's youthful spirit in his old age.

I. ii. 199. *Sirrah.* The ordinary form of address to children and servants; here, a sign of Poins's undue familiarity with the Prince.

I. ii. 206. *the third,* i.e., Falstaff. Shakespeare's inaccuracy in unimportant details is well illustrated here. He has just mentioned four robbers (ll. 180-181), and now implies, at least, that there are to be but three. The phrase 'those men that we have already waylaid' (ll. 181-182) is also inaccurate and misleading. Falstaff and his three followers both waylay and rob the men, after Hal and Poins have withdrawn. But Shakespeare wrote primarily for the stage, and not for the closet, and inaccuracies of this sort are not apparent on the stage.

I. iii. 36. *milliner.* In Shakespeare's time, milliners, i.e., dealers in women's clothes from Milan, were, for the most part, men.

I. iii. 56. *God save the mark.* A deprecatory expression, of obscure origin, used when reference is made to an unpleasant subject.

I. iii. 137. *Bolingbroke.* King Henry is referred to by many names during the course of the play. Before his accession he was commonly known as Henry of Bolingbroke, from the fact that he was born in Bolingbroke castle in Lincolnshire. He also bore the titles Earl of Derby, Duke of Hereford, and, after his father's death, Duke of Lancaster.

I. iii. 145-146. The following genealogical table will help to make clear this question of the succession to the English throne:

Edward III (1327-1377)

Edward, Prince of Wales ('the Black Prince') d. 1376	Lionel, Duke of Clarence	John of Gaunt, Duke of Lancaster
Richard II (1377-1399)	Philippa, m. Edmund Mortimer, Earl of March	Henry IV (1399-1414)

Roger M., Earl of March	Edmund M.	Elizabeth M. m. Harry Percy

Edmund Mortimer, Earl
of March, d. 1424

Shakespeare follows the chroniclers in confusing
Edmund Mortimer, the son of Philippa, with
Edmund Mortimer, the son of Roger. It was Roger
Mortimer who was King Richard's heir, and was so
proclaimed in the October Parliament of 1385. At
his death in 1398, one year before King Richard's,
his seven-year-old son succeeded to his claim. But
it was the elder Edmund, brother to Roger, who
fought Glendower and married his daughter. Hotspur's brother-in-law, therefore, was not heir to the
throne. The heir, as the table shows, was the nephew
of Lady Percy, and in III. i. 195 Mortimer refers to
Lady Percy as 'my aunt Percy.' Here (l. 156), and
in l. 80, Mortimer is represented as Hotspur's
brother-in-law.

I. iii. 245. *York.* Edmund of Langley, Duke of
York, younger brother to John of Gaunt, uncle to

King Richard and King Henry. Richard had appointed York regent of England during the king's absence in Ireland. Richard had previously exiled Henry, and the latter chose this period of the king's absence from his realm to return and claim his father's estates, which had been unjustly confiscated by Richard to pay for this same Irish expedition. Henry was met at Ravenspurgh, on the coast of Yorkshire, by Northumberland; at Doncaster, in southern Yorkshire, by Worcester; and finally at Berkeley Castle, in Gloucestershire, by Hotspur. The interview between Hotspur and Henry, from which Hotspur quotes in his next speech, is presented in Shakespeare's *Richard II*, II. iii.

I. iii. 271. *the Lord Scroop.* One of the adherents of King Richard, executed by order of Henry; see *Richard II*, III. ii.

II. i. 2. *Charles' Wain.* Probably a corruption of churl's wain' or 'countryman's wagon,' the name given to the constellation which is now known as the Great Bear.

II. i. 10. *next,* the old superlative of *nigh,* of which *near* was the comparative. Cf. III. i. 263.

II. i. 17. There is an old superstition, referred to in Pliny's *Natural History*, ix. 47, that fishes are infested with fleas. Cf. l. 23.

II. i. 28. *Charing-cross,* in Shakespeare's time a village on the road from London to Westminster; now in the heart of Greater London.

II. i. 67. *Saint Nicholas,* a popular saint in the Roman and Russian Churches, now familiarly known as Santa Claus, was the patron saint of scholars, children, parish clerks, travellers, sailors, and pawnbrokers. His aid was invoked by travellers to protect them from perils of the road, especially from robbers.

II. i. 81 ff. *foot-land-rakers,* foot-pads; *long-staff*

sixpenny strikers, fellows who would knock a man down to get sixpence from him; *mustachio-purple-hued malt worms,* fellows whose moustaches are so constantly immersed in ale that they have become purple; *tranquillity,* people who live at ease; *great oneyers,* great ones (with a play on the words *one* and *own* which were pronounced alike); *such as can hold in,* such as can keep their own counsel (an accomplishment which Gadshill seems to find it difficult to imitate).

II. i. 94.   Greasing of boots to make them water-proof was called 'liquoring' them; the play on the word here is obvious.

II. i. 96. *receipt of fern-seed.* According to popular superstition, fern-seed was visible only on Saint John's Eve (June 23), and those who gathered it then, according to a certain rite, were themselves rendered invisible.

II. ii. 2.   *frets like a gummed velvet.*   Velvet stiffened with gum very soon chafed.

II. iii. 1.   The writer of this letter is not specified.

II. iii. 37.   I could divide myself into two parts and then fight with myself.

II. iii. 41.   *Kate.*   The actual Hotspur's wife's name was Elizabeth, not Kate; cf. genealogical table on page 118.   Shakespeare seems to have had a peculiar fondness for the name Kate.

II. iii. 50-51. Why have you allowed musing and melancholy, which have made you 'thick-eyed,' i.e., blind to all outward things, to make you forget your attention to me, which is my 'treasure'?

II. iii. 58.   The basilisk cannon was named from the fabulous monster whose look was reputed to kill. The culverin is also named from a serpent.

II. iii. 98.   *crowns.* Used quibblingly: broken

heads, or damaged coin, still in circulation, 'passing current.'

II. iv. 21. *tinker.* Tinkers were famous for their capacity for strong drink and for their picturesque vocabulary.

II. iv. 59. *Michaelmas.* The feast of St. Michael, September 29; one of the four quarter days of the English business year.

II. iv. 83 ff. Hal here talks nonsense, with the express purpose of confusing Francis still more.

II. iv. 125. *brawn.* The fleshy part of the body, especially the calf of the leg or the buttocks. Falstaff is again referred to as a 'brawn' in *Henry IV, Pt. II.* I. i. 19: 'Harry Monmouth's brawn, the hulk Sir John.'

II. iv. 135. *Titan.* The sun. Mispunctuation has resulted in making this speech of Prince Hal's obscure in most modern editions. The phrase 'pitiful-hearted Titan' is obviously parenthetical, as Warburton first suggested, and the clause beginning 'that melted' refers to 'butter.'

II. iv. 149. *weaver.* Elizabethan weavers were, for the most part, 'psalm-singing Puritans,' who had fled to England from the religious persecutions in the Low Countries.

II. iv. 242. *points.* Falstaff refers to the points of swords. Poins, in his reply, quibblingly interprets points in another sense, namely, *garters.*

II. iv. 250. *Kendal-green.* A dark green woolen cloth made at Kendal in Westmoreland; the traditional costume of Robin Hood.

II. iv. 266. *strappado.* A military punishment which consisted of fastening a rope under the arms of the offender, drawing him up by a pulley to the top of a high beam, and then suddenly letting him down with a jerk.

II. iv. 268. *reasons.* A play on the words *reasons* and *raisins,* which were pronounced alike.

II. iv. 325. *royal.* A royal was 10s.; a noble 6s. 8d.

II. iv. 355-362. Bardolph becomes angry and adopts a threatening attitude. 'My red face,' he implies, 'portends *choler* (*anger*).' Hal finds it merely a sign of *a hot liver* (caused by drinking) and an empty purse (also caused by drink). When Bardolph insists that it is *choler,* Hal quibblingly interprets *choler* as *collar,* and suggests that if his face were rightly taken, it would be taken by a halter.

II. iv. 430. *King Cambyses.* A ranting bombastic tragedy by Thomas Preston (1570). Line 436 shows that Falstaff knew more than the name of the play, one line of which reads: '(*At this tale tolde let the Queene weep.*)

Queene: These wordes to hear makes stilling teares
    issue from christal eyes.'

II. iv. 443. Falstaff may be referring to the Hostess as a pint-pot always well filled with ticklebrain, or he may be using tickle-brain not in its technical sense, but merely as an appropriate word for describing the flighty character of the Hostess.

II. iv. 444 ff. Falstaff is here burlesquing the somewhat pompous and artificial style of King Henry, and Shakespeare is, at the same time, burlesquing the fashionable and artificial prose style of his own contemporaries, known as Euphuism. This style was exemplified in John Lyly's *Euphues* (1578-1580), and its chief characteristics are: (1) The constant use of antithesis, (2) The use of alliteration to emphasize the antithetic clauses, (3) The frequent use of a long string of similes all relating to the same subject, often taken from the fabulous qualities ascribed to plants, animals, and minerals, (4) The constant use of rhetorical questions, (5) Frequent

quotation of proverbs. Falstaff's first figure is taken
directly from *Euphues* (ed. Bond, vol. I, p. 196):
'Though the Camomill the more it is trodden and
pressed downe, the more it spreadeth, yet the Violet
the oftner it is handeled and touched, the sooner it
withereth and decayeth.' The following passages
are good examples of Euphuism (Bond, I. 222):
'Though thou haue eaten the seedes of Rockatte
which breede incontinencie, yet haue I chewed the
leafe Cresse which mainteineth modestie. Though
thou beare in thy bosome the hearbe Araxa most
noisome to virginitie, yet haue I the stone that
groweth in the mounte Tmolus, the vpholder of
chastitie.' 'Well doth he know that the glass once
crased will with the least clappe be cracked . . .
But can Euphues conuince me of fleetinge, seeing for
his sake I breake my fidelitie? Can he condemne
me of disloyaltie, when he is the only cause of my
dislyking? May he condemn me of trecherye, who
hath this testimony as tryall of my good will? Doth
he not remember that . . . though the Spyder poyson
the Flye, she cannot infect the Bee? That though
I have bene light to Philautus, yet I may be louely
to Euphues?' (Bond, I. 205-206.)

II. iv. 486-487. Falstaff is comparing himself with
the thinnest things he can think of, a young sucking
rabbit, or a hare hung up in a poulterer's shop.

II. iv. 495. *I'll tickle ye*, etc. This is obviously
an aside to Hal, and not part of Falstaff's speech in
his rôle of Prince. As he begins his performance, he
whispers to Hal, 'My acting of the part of a young
prince will tickle you, i' faith.'

II. iv. 504. *Manningtree ox*. Manningtree is a
town in Essex, famous for its fairs at which oxen
were roasted whole.

II. iv. 527. *Pharaoh's lean kine*. Cf. Genesis 41.
19.

II. iv. 547-549. There are two possible interpretations of this speech. The first (Malone's) is that Falstaff is referring here to the real danger which now confronts them; the second (Wright's) is that Falstaff, all absorbed in 'playing out the play,' waves the Hostess aside and continues his defence of himself. If we accept the first interpretation, we may paraphrase Falstaff's speech as follows: 'Dost thou hear that, Hal? Don't yield to one of your mad impulses now, and make light of a serious matter.' Hal's reply would tend to support this interpretation.

II. iv. 557-558. Falstaff hides behind the curtain which divided the outer from the inner stage in the Elizabethan theatre; the others 'walk above,' i.e., on the balcony above the inner stage.

III. i. 100. *the best of all my land.* All Lincolnshire and part of Nottinghamshire. See map.

III. i. 148-152. The division of the kingdom was made by the conspirators, according to Holinshed, 'through a foolish credit given to a vain prophecy' that Henry was a moldwarp (a mole) whose kingdom should be divided among a wolf, a dragon, and a lion. This cryptic prophecy was attributed to Merlin, and is referred to in *The Mirror for Magistrates* (1559):

And for to set us hereon more agog,
A prophet came (a vengeaunce take them all)
Affirming Henry to be Gog-magog,
Whom Merlin doth a mouldwarp ever call,
Accursed of God, that must be brought in thrall
By a wulf, a dragon, and a lyon strong,
Which shuld devide his kingdome them amonge.

Hotspur evidently has not shared in the 'foolish credit' given to the 'vain prophecy' and his only memory of the discussion is that Glendower talked a lot of Celtic nonsense.

III. i. 200-203. Mortimer seems to be trying to say that though he does not understand his wife's speech, he understands her looks, and that he is 'too perfect' in the language of tears (i.e., 'the pretty Welsh' which she pours down from her swollen eyes). So near to tears is the bridegroom himself that shame alone prevents his answering his wife's tears with tears.

III. i. 256. *Finsbury*. Archery grounds just outside of London, a favorite resort of respectable middle-class citizens.

III. i. 260. *velvet-guards*. Velvet trimmings; hence women that wear such finery, notably wives of aldermen.

III. i. 263. *tailor*. Tailors, like weavers (cf. II. iv. 149 n.), were noted for singing at their work.

III. ii. 50. I assumed, or took upon myself, a heavenly graciousness of bearing.

III. ii. 62. *carded*. To card was to mix different kinds of drink; so King Richard mixed his high state and dignity with baseness.

III. ii. 99. Hal's claim to the crown is shadowy compared with Hotspur's, for Hal's claim is that of inheritance from a usurper who has been rewarded with the crown for his services to the state; whereas Hotspur's claim is that of efficient public service, performed by himself.

III. iii. 10. *brewer's horse*. The point of this comparison lies probably in the fact that a brewer's horse carries good liquor on his back, instead of in his belly.

III. iii. 35. It was the fashion to wear, as a *memento mori*, reminder of death, a ring or pin on the stone of which was engraved a skull and crossbones.

III. iii. 36. See St. Luke's Gospel, 16. 19-31.

III. iii. 40. Cf. Psalm 104. 4: Who maketh his angels spirits; his ministers a flaming fire.

III. iii. 60. *Partlet.* The name of the hen in the famous story of the Cock and the. Fox; cf. Chaucer's *Nonne Preestes Tale.* The hen-like characteristics of the hostess are apparent in the conversation immediately following.

III. iii. 128-129. *Maid Marian.* The mistress of Robin Hood, often impersonated by a man in the morris-dances, in which she was traditionally a rather disreputable person. 'As regards womanliness,' says Falstaff to the hostess, 'in comparison with you, Maid Marian is as respectable a person as the wife of the deputy-alderman of this ward.'

III. iii. 181. *injuries.* 'As the pocketing of injuries was a common phrase, I suppose the Prince calls the contents of Falstaff's pockets injuries.' (Steevens.) Cf. 182-183.

III. iii. 205. *unwashed hands.* Without stopping to wash your hands, i.e., at once; or, possibly, without any over-fastidious scruples.

III. iii. 228. *drum.* Used here in the sense of rallying-point or recruiting station.

IV. i. 4-5. Another figurative expression referring to coinage; cf. II. iii. 97-99. 'Your fame would circulate more widely than that of any soldier of this season's coinage.'

IV. i. 53. 'Whereas now we have the pleasant prospect of future possession.'

IV. i. 56. 'The comfort of having something to fall back upon.'

IV. i. 98-99. 'All plumed like ostriches that flap their wings in the wind like eagles that have lately bathed.' The obscurity of this passage is caused by the double comparison, of men with ostriches, and ostriches with eagles. Bate means literally to beat the wings impatiently and flutter away from a perch. Three ostrich plumes have always been the cognizance of the Prince of Wales.

IV. i. 100. *images.* The reference is probably to the festival robes which adorn the images of the saints on holy days.

IV. i. 111-112. 'Your praise of him causes me greater pain than the ague in the Spring.'

IV. i. 114. *maid.* Bellona, goddess of war.

IV. ii. 3. *Sutton-Co'fil'.* Sutton-Coldfield, a town twenty-four miles northwest of Coventry.

IV. ii. 6. 'makes an angel, or ten shillings, that I have spent.'

IV. ii. 18-19. 'Whose banns had been twice published,' i.e., they were to be married immediately.

IV. ii. 37. St. Luke's Gospel, 15. 15-16.

V. i. 13. *old limbs.* The historical King Henry was thirty-seven years old at the time of the battle of Shrewsbury; the historical Hotspur was forty; and the historical Prince Hal seventeen. The King of Shakespeare's play is, however, an elderly man, and Hotspur and Hal are both young. I. i. 87-89 shows that Shakespeare regarded his two youthful heroes as of the same age; and III. ii. 112-113 would indicate that they were very young.

V. i. 60-61. The cuckoo frequently lays her eggs in the hedge-sparrow's nest; and the hedge-sparrow brings up the young cuckoos, until they have 'grown to such a bulk' that they destroy their foster-parents. Cf. *Lear*, I. iv. 235:

> The hedge-sparrow fed the cuckoo so long
> That it had it head, bit off by it young.

V. i. 127-128. There is probably a pun here on the words death and debt which were pronounced alike.

V. iii. 46. *Turk Gregory.* Editors all agree that Falstaff here refers to Pope Gregory VII, Hildebrand, who, as a friar, was famous for military exploits. Attempts to explain the appellation Turk are not very satisfactory. Falstaff perhaps has in mind the phrase 'to fight like a Turk.'

V. iii. 58. Another pun. The -ie- of pierce was pronounced like the -e- of Percy.

V. iv. 65. A reference to Ptolemaic astronomy, according to which each planet was fixed in a crystal sphere with which it revolved.

V. iv. 81-83. 'The glory of the Prince wounds his *thoughts;* but *thought,* being dependent on *life,* must cease with it, and will soon be at an end. *Life,* on which *thought* depends, is itself of no great value, being the *fool* and sport of *time;* of *time,* which, with all its dominion over sublunary things, *must* itself at last be stopped.' (Johnson.)

V. iv. 114. *termagant.* Name of one of the fabled idols worshipped by Mohammedans, according to the Mediæval Romance.

APPENDIX A

VARIANTS

The text used in this edition is that of Craig's Oxford Shakespeare (Oxford University Press), which follows, almost invariably, the First Quarto, the best early text of *Henry IV, Part I*. The stage-directions are not those of the Oxford Shakespeare, but are for the most part from either the First Quarto or the First Folio; stage-directions which are bracketed are modern.

Occasionally the Oxford Shakespeare departs from the reading of the First Quarto, and substitutes an inferior reading from the First Folio. In such cases I have restored the Quarto readings, as noted below.

I have taken the title of the play from the First Folio. The First Quarto title, which omits the phrase 'The first part,' is as follows:

THE | HISTORY OF | HENRIE THE | FOURTH; | With the battell at Shrewsburie | *betweene the King and Lord* | Henry Percy, surnamed Henrie Hotspur of the North | *With the humorous conceits of Sir* | Iohn Falstaffe.

In the *Dramatis Personæ*, the Oxford Shakespeare omits the name of Francis, although in all stage-directions and before speeches it uses the name Francis instead of the word 'Drawer' which is used in Quartos and Folios.

The list of my departures from the Oxford text follows:

YALE	OXFORD
I. i. 28 now is twelve months Q1	is a twelvemonth F1
I. i. 42 A hundred Q1	And a hundred F1
I. i. 49 with other, did, Q1	with other like F1

I. iii. 71 Whate'er Lord Q1	Whatever F1
I. iii. 83 that Q1	the F1
I. iii. 124 you will Q1	you'll F1
II. i. 38 and 44 lantern Q1, F1	lanthorn
II. ii. 57 Bardolph, what news? Q1 F1	*Bard.* What news?
II. iv. 163 by the Lord, I'll stab thee Q1	I'll stab thee F1
II. iv. 379 O, Glendower Q1, F1	Owen Glendower
II. iv. 499 an old fat man Q1	a fat old man F1
III. i. 10 wisheth Q1, F1	wishes
III. iii. 18 not—above	not above Q1, F1
III. iii. 21 borrowed—three	borrowed three Q1, F1
III. iii. 29 lantern Q1, F1	lanthorn
III. iii. 194 pacified still Q1, F1	pacified. Still!
III. iii. 219 Peto Q1, F1	Poins
IV. i. 98 with the wind Q1, F1	wing the wind
V. iv. 100 ignominy Q1	ignomy F1

APPENDIX B

SOURCES

The sources of the serious plot of both parts of Shakespeare's *Henry IV* are (1) the 1587 edition of *The Chronicles of England, Scotland, and Ireland* by Raphael Holinshed 'of Bromecote in the County of Warr(wick)'; and (2) either Samuel Daniel's poem, *The Civill Wars of England* (1595) or some lost poem, play, or chronicle followed by both Daniel and Shakespeare.

The source of the comic plot is a crude and slight chronicle play called *The Famous Victories of Henry V*, first acted in 1588, licensed in 1594, and published in 1598.

Selections from Holinshed's Account of the Battle of Shrewsbury

The next daie in the morning earlie, being the even of Marie Magdalene (July 21. 1403), they set their battells in order on both sides, and now, whilest the warriors looked when the token of battell should be given, the abbat of Shrewesburie, and one of the clerks of the privie seale, were sent from the king vnto the Persies, to offer them pardon, if they would come to any reasonable agreement. By their persuasions, the lord Henrie Persie began to give ear vnto the kings offers, & so sent with them his vncle the earle of Worcester, to declare vnto the king the causes of those troubles. . . .

It was reported for a truth, that now when the king had condescended vnto all that was reasonable at his hands to be required, and seemed to humble himself

more than was meet for his estate, the earle of
Worcester vpon his return to his nephue made
relation cleane contrarie to that the king had said,
in such sort that he set his nephues hart more in
displeasure toward the king than euer it was before;
driving him by that means to fight whether he would
or not. . . .

And forthwith the lord Persie, as a capteine of
high courage, began to exhort the capteines and
souldiers to prepare themselves to battell, sith the
matter was grown to that point, that by no meanes
it could be avoided, "so that," said he, "this daie
shall either bring vs all to advancement & honor, or
else if it shall chance vs to be overcome, shall deliuer
us from the kings spitefull malice and cruell disdaine:
for plaieng the men, as we ought to doo, better it is
to die in battell for the commonwealths cause, than
through cowardlike feare to prolong life, which after
shall be taken from us by the sentence of the
enimie. . . .

Then suddenlie blew the trumpets, the kings part
crieng, "St. George! Upon them!" the adversaries
cried *"Esperance! Persie!"* and so the two armies
furiouslie ioined. . . .

The prince that daie holpe his father like a lustie
yoong gentleman; for although he was hurt in the
face with an arrow, so that diuerse noblemen, that
were aboute him, would have conveyed him foorth
from the field, yet he would not suffer them so to
doo, least his departure from amongst his men might
happilie have stricken some feare into their harts:
and so without regard of his hurt, he continued with
his men, and never ceassed either to fight where the
battell was most hot, or to incourage his men where
it seemed most need.

SELECTIONS FROM DANIEL'S CIVILL WARS, BOOK IV

(The battle of Shrewsbury)

No. 37

And yet, undaunted Hotspur, seeing the King
So neere arriv'd; leaving the work in hand, . . .
Brings on his army, eger vnto fight;
And plac't the same before the king in sight.

No. 38

"This day (saith he) my valiant trusty friends,
"Whatever it shall give, shal glory give;
"This day, with honor, frees our state, or ends
"Our misery with fame, that still shal live:
"And doo but thinke, how well the same he spends,
"Who spends his blood, his Country to relieve.
"What? Have we hands, and shall we servile bee?
"Why were swordes made? but, to preserve men free.

No. 45

Forthwith, began these fury-moving sounds,
The notes, of wrath, the musicke brought from Hell,
The ratling drums (which trumpets voyce confounds)
The cryes, th' incouragements, the shouting shrill;
That, all about, the beaten ayre rebounds
Confused thundring-murmurs horrible. . . .

No. 48

There, lo that new-appearing glorious starre,
Wonder of armes, the terror of the field,
Young Henrie, labouring where the stoutest are,
And even the stoutest forceth backe to yeeld. . . .

No. 52

And never worthy Prince a day did quit
With greater hazard, and with more renowne
Than thou didst, mighty *Henrie, in this fight;
Which onely made thee owner of thine owne. . . .

No. 53

And deare it cost, and much good blood is shed
To purchase thee, a saving victorie:

---

* The King.

Great Stafford, thy high Constable, lyes dead,
With Shorly, Clifton, Gawsell, Calverly,
And many more; whose brave deaths witnessed
Their noble valour and fidelitie:
And many more had left their dearest bloud
Behind, that day, had Hotspur longer stood.

No. 54

But he, as Dowglas, with a furie ledde,
Rushing into the thickest woods of speares,
And brakes of swordes, still laying at the Head
(The life of th' army) whiles he nothing feares
Or spares his owne, comes all invironed
With multitude of power, that overbeares
His manly worth: who yeeldes not in his fall;
But fighting dyes, and dying kils withal.

SELECTION FROM THE FAMOUS VICTORIES OF HENRY V

The following is the first conversation between Prince Hal and Falstaff (Sir John Oldcastle):

Enter Sir Iohn Old-Castle.

Hen. 5. How now sir Iohn Old-Castle,
    What newes with you?
Ioh. Old. I am glad to see your grace at libertie,*
    I was come, I, to visit you in prison.
Hen. 5. To visit me? Didst thou not know that I
    am a Princes son. . . But I tell you, sirs,
    when I am king we will have no such things.
    But, my lads, if the old king, my father, were
    dead, we should all be kings.
Ioh. Old. Hee is a goode olde man, God take him to
    his mercy the sooner.
Hen. 5. But, Ned, so soone as I am King, the first
    thing I will do, shal be to put my lord chief

---

* The Prince had just been committed to the Fleet for striking the Lord Chief Justice.

Justice out of office. And thou shalt be my
Lord chiefe Justice of England.

Ned. Shall I be Lord chiefe Justice?
By gogs wounds, ile be the bravest Lord
chiefe Justice
That ever was in England.

Hen. 5. Thou shalt hang none but picke purses and
horse stealers, and such base-minded vil-
laines. But that fellow that will stand by
the high way side couragiously with his sword
and buckler and take a purse, that fellow
give him commendations, beside that send
him to me and I will give him an annual
pension out of my Exchequer.

C

APPENDIX C

THE HISTORY OF THE PLAY

1. DATE OF COMPOSITION

King Henry IV, Part I, was apparently written in the year 1596-1597, when Shakespeare was in his thirty-third year. He had probably already produced nine successful plays, among them *Romeo and Juliet* and *The Merchant of Venice.* The year 1596 had witnessed the English expedition to Spain and the destruction of the city of Cadiz; the year 1597 saw the destruction of the second Spanish Armada. English patriotism never found nobler expression than in the historical plays of Shakespeare written during these years of national trial and endeavour.

2. EARLY EDITIONS

The popularity of this play is attested by the large number of early editions, no less than six appearing before the publication of the first Folio in 1623. The first Quarto appeared in 1598, and was followed by others in 1599, 1604, 1608, 1613, and 1622. The first Quarto furnishes the best text. The text of the first Folio was apparently based upon the fifth Quarto.

3. SIR JOHN OLDCASTLE AND SIR JOHN FALSTAFF

In Shakespeare's first version of the play he evidently retained the name Oldcastle for the fat knight who attended the Prince. Hal's pun, 'my old lad of the castle' (I. ii.) bears witness to this, as does the metrical imperfection in the line

·Away good Ned, Falstaff sweats to death (II. ii.)
which would be corrected by the substitution of the
word Oldcastle for Falstaff. In the first Quarto of
Henry IV, Part II, the prefix *Old.* is found instead
of *Fal.* before Falstaff's speech in I. ii. 137, and in the
Epilogue to this play the author explicitly states that
the Falstaff of the play is not the Oldcastle who 'died
a martyr.'

Oldcastle was a famous Lollard, and according to
tradition many Elizabethan Protestants protested
against Shakespeare's 'degradation' of an honorable
name, and 'some of that family being then remain-
ing, the Queen was pleased to command him to alter
it.' It is at least a singular coincidence that Shakespeare substituted the name of a Lollard sympathizer,
Sir John Fastolfe, in slightly disguised form. The
Falstaff of the play bears no resemblance, save in
name, to either Sir John Oldcastle or Sir John
Fastolfe.

4. STAGE HISTORY

Of the first performances and the first players of
Henry IV no records are extant; but the large number
of contemporary references add their' testimony to
the fact of the play's popularity. Ben Jonson
alludes to the fatness of Sir John Falstaff in *Every
Man out of his Humour,* and in Beaumont and
Fletcher's *Knight of the Burning Pestle,* Ralph, the
apprentice, when asked to 'speak a huffing part,'
declaims Hotspur's speech on honor, with variations.
Shakespeare's chief rivals, the Lord Admiral's players, in 1599 paid him the compliment of producing a
play of their own on *The Life of Sir John Oldcastle;*
and even during the period of the Commonwealth,
Puritan legislation failed to prevent the clandestine
performance of a farcical abridgment of Shakespeare's play, known as *The Bouncing Knight.*

John Lowin (1576-1659) is the earliest actor whose name is associated with the play. James Wright in his *Historia Histrionica* (1699) says that 'before the wars' Lowin acted Falstaff 'with mighty applause.' Lowin seems to have joined Shakespeare's company in 1603, six or seven years after the probable date of the first performance of *Henry IV*.

This play was one of the first to be revived publicly after the Restoration. Pepys first saw it in December, 1660, and was disappointed,—'my expectation being too great, . . . and my having a book I believe did spoil it a little.' The next spring, however, Pepys saw it again, and pronounced it 'a good play.' In November, 1667, and September, 1668, Pepys attended performances again, and 'contrary to expectation was pleased in nothing more than in Cartwright's speaking of Falstaff's speech about "What is Honour?"'

During the seventies John Lacey succeeded Cartwright in the rôle of Falstaff; and in 1682, the year after Lacey's death, at the time of the union of the King's and the Duke's players, the great Thomas Betterton appeared as Hotspur. Eighteen years later, at the age of sixty-five, Betterton appeared as Falstaff 'which drew all the town more than any new play produced of late. . . . The critics allow that Betterton has hit the humour of Falstaff better than any that have aimed at it before, . . . though he lacks the waggery of Estcourt, the drollery of Harper, and the salaciousness of Jack Evans.' (*Genest*, II. 381; V. 596.) Six notable Falstaffs in one generation is a record of which the seventeenth century may be proud.

Betterton's acting version of the play was published in 1700. *Genest* notes that he 'judiciously retains' the conversation of Falstaff and the Prince in Act II, and also the first scene in Act III, although he omits the character of Lady Mortimer.

The obvious inference to be drawn from *Genest's*
opening remark is indeed astounding, namely, that
it had been the custom, before Betterton's time, to
cut the great Boar's Head Tavern scene. But it
was after Betterton's time that, according to *Genest*,
a 'happy (*sic*) addition' was made to Falstaff's
speech which begins 'By the Lord, I knew ye as
well as he that made ye' by prefixing the question
'Do ye think that I did not know ye?' This sin-
gularly infelicitous addition to Shakespeare's text
was retained by Sir Herbert Tree in his performance
of the Boar's Head Tavern scene at the Shakespeare
Tercentenary Festival in the New Amsterdam
Theatre, New York, in April, 1916.

Verbruggen was Betterton's Hotspur, and according to *Genest* (II. 381) he was 'nature without
extravagance, and freedom without licentiousness,—
he was vociferous without bellowing.' The inference
to be drawn with respect to former performances is
again interesting.

Twenty other actors are known to have played
Falstaff between 1700 and 1750, and the play-bills
of twenty performances of *Henry IV, Part I*, between
1706 and 1826 are in existence. Six of these performances were at the Haymarket, seven at Drury
Lane, two at Lincoln's Inn Fields, and five at Covent
Garden.

Garrick first appeared as Hotspur at the Covent
Garden performance in 1746, his great rival, Quin,
appearing as Falstaff, a rôle in which he had made
himself a great name eight years before. We are
told that 'the advantage was greatly on Quin's side,
as the part of Hotspur was not suited to Garrick's
figure or style of acting.'

Henderson was the great Falstaff of the latter half
of the eighteenth century, and played at the Haymarket, Drury Lane, and Covent Garden. He is
said to have made Falstaff 'neither very vulgar nor

very polite.' An entirely unique performance must
have been that of 1786 when Mrs. Webb appeared
as Falstaff in a 'benefit' for herself.

In the 1824 production at Covent Garden, Charles
Kemble appeared as Falstaff. 'He endeavored to
rescue the part from coarseness. In the presence of
the King and in the conversation with Westmoreland,
he invested it with gentility and courtly bearing.'
The Drury Lane production two years later was made
notable by the appearance of Macready as Hotspur.

A popular Falstaff of the early nineteenth century
was Bartley, who made his first appearance in the
rôle in 1815. 'His success was equal to his most
sanguine expectations, and richly merited.' Bartley
made a triumphal tour of America in 1818-1819, and
gave instruction in reading and elocution in many
American colleges. In 'Hertford,' the capital of
Connecticut, he and his accomplished wife were
arrested for indulging in dramatic readings, one
Ebenezer Huntington, a Puritanical Attorney General, having resurrected one of Connecticut's famous
blue laws for this purpose.

Since Bartley's farewell performance in 1852, there
have been few revivals of *Henry IV*. For two cen-
turies the play was revived in almost every decade;
since 1850 it has been practically ignored. In recent
years it has formed part of the repertoire of Sir
Herbert Tree and of Sir Francis Benson's company
at the Stratford Memorial Theatre. Miss Julia Mar-
lowe appeared as Prince Hal in an abridgement of the
two parts of the play in New York in 1895-1896, with
William F. Owen as Falstaff. Professor Brander
Matthews has recorded some excellent stage business
of Owen's in an essay on Stage Traditions, published
in *Shakespearean Studies*, Columbia University Press,
1916. The play has been revived in England and
America by University Dramatic Associations, at
Cambridge in 1886 and at Yale in 1906.

BIBLIOGRAPHY

I. FALSTAFF.

1. Maurice Morgann: *An Essay on the Dramatic Character of Sir John Falstaff*. London, 1777.
2. William Maginn: *Shakespeare Papers. Falstaff*. New York, 1856.
3. E. E. Stoll: *Falstaff*. Modern Philology, October, 1914. (Full of useful information, but a notable example of the insufficiency of mere "scientific" treatment of literature.)

II. PRINCE HAL.

1. A. C. Bradley: *Oxford Lectures on Poetry. The Rejection of Falstaff*. London, 1909.

III. GENERAL CRITICISM.

1. William Hazlitt: *The Characters of Shakespeare's Plays*. London, 1817.
2. Henry N. Hudson: *Shakespeare, his Life, Art, and Characters*. Boston, 1872.
3. Edward Dowden: *Shakespeare, a Critical Study*. London, 1880.
4. George Brandes: *William Shakespeare. A Critical Study*. Translated into English by William Archer. London, 1897.
5. John Masefield: *William Shakespeare*. New York, 1911.
6. Stopford Brooke: *Ten More Plays of Shakespeare*. London, 1913.

IV. MISCELLANEOUS.

1. Beverley E. Warner: *English History in Shakespeare's Plays*. New York, 1894.
2. Brander Matthews: *Stage Traditions* in *Shakespeare Studies* by the English Faculty of Columbia University. New York, 1916.

INDEX OF WORDS GLOSSED

(Figures in full-faced type refer to page-numbers)

stock-fish: **45** (II. iv. 275)
stole: **68** (III. ii. 50)
stomach: **33** (II. iii. 46)
stout: **109** (V. iv. 93)
straight: **17** (I. iii. 126)
strait: **91** (IV. iii. 79)
strappado: **45** (II. iv. 266)
stronds: **1** (I. i. 4)
subornation: **18** (I. iii. 163)
sue his livery: **90** (IV. iii. 62)
sufferances: **95** (V. i. 51)
suggestion: **90** (IV. iii. 51)
suits: **7** (I. ii. 81)
sullen: **12** (I. ii. 234)
summer-house: **62** (III. i. 163)
Sutton-Co'fil': **85** (IV. ii. 3)
sword and buckler: **21** (I. iii. 230)

tailor: **66** (III. i. 263)
take it upon: **36** (II. iv. 9)
take me with you: **53** (II. iv. 513)
taken with the manner: **47** (II. iv. 350)
tall: **15** (I. iii. 62)
tallow-ketch: **44** (II. iv. 256)
target: **43** (II. iv. 228)
task me to my word: **80** (IV. i. 9)
task'd: **91** (IV. iii. 92)
tasking: **100** (V. ii. 50)
tench: **24** (II. i. 17)
termagant: **109** (V. iv. 114)
tickle-brain: **50** (II. iv. 443)
time: **67** (III. ii. 36)
tinker: **37** (II. iv. 21)
Titan: **41** (II. iv. 135)
toss: **87** (IV. ii. 72)
trace: **58** (III. i. 48)
trenching: **1** (I. i. 7)
trim: **84** (IV. i. 113)

tristful: **50** (II. iv. 439)
Troyans: **26** (II. i. 77)
trunk of humours: **52** (II. iv. 501)
Turk Gregory: **104** (V. iii. 46)

underskinker: **37** (II. iv. 26)
uneven: **3** (I. i. 50)
unsorted: **32** (II. iii. 15)
unwashed: **79** (III. iii. 205)
unyok'd: **12** (I. ii. 218)
uttered: **4** (I. i. 107)

valued: **72** (III. ii. 177)
vassal: **70** (III. ii. 124)
velvet-guards: **65** (III. i. 260)
vile: **69** (III. ii. 87)
virtue: **41** (II. iv. 134)
vizards: **9** (I. ii. 141)

wait on us: **97** (V. i. 111)
want: **81** (IV. i. 44)
wanton: **64** (III. i. 214)
wanton time: **95** (V. i. 50)
wards: **12** (I. ii. 211)
warm: **86** (IV. ii. 19)
watering: **36** (II. iv. 17)
weaver: **41** (II. iv. 149)
well-respected: **88** (IV. iii. 10)
Welsh hook: **48** (II. iv. 378)
whoreson: **30** (II. ii. 92)
wild: **25** (II. i. 60)
wilful-blame: **62** (III. i. 176)
wind: **84** (IV. i. 109)
withers: **24** (II. i. 8)
worship: **71** (III. ii. 151)
wrung: **24** (II. i. 8)

yeoman's: **85** (IV. ii. 16)
York: **21** (I. iii. 245)
younker: **75** (III. iii. 91)

'Zounds: **8** (I. ii. 112)

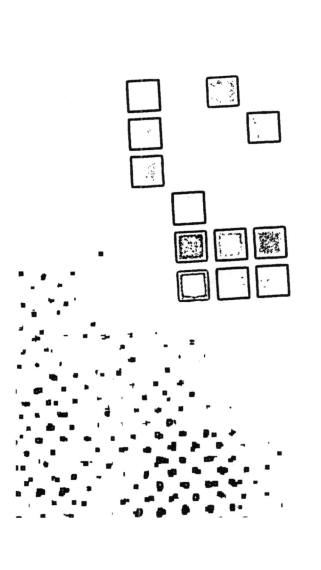